CHOOSE YE THIS DAY

Daily Inspirations from the Old Testament

CHOOSE YE THIS DAY

Daily Inspirations from the Old Testament

ED J. PINEGAR & RICHARD J. ALLEN

Covenant Communications, Inc.

Cover image *Job and His Family* © Greg Olsen. By arrangement with Mill Pond Press, Inc. Venice, Florida, 34292. For information on art prints by Greg Olsen, please contact Mill Pond Press at 1-800-535-0331. All interior images © Robert T. Barrett.

Cover design copyrighted 2005 by Covenant Communications, Inc.

Published by Covenant Communications, Inc.
American Fork, Utah

Printed in the United States of America
First Printing: September 2005

21 20 19 18 17 16 15 14 13   10 9 8 7 6 5 4 3

ISBN 1-59811-016-0

Preface

Over the vast landscape of the Old Testament, the spiritual eye can survey with clarity the divine agenda unfolding in all of its magnificence: from the dawn of earth's creation to the eve of the Savior's ministry; from the foundation of the Abrahamic era to the late prophetic pronouncements of Jeremiah, Ezekiel, and Daniel; from the sonorous outpourings of David's psalms to the soaring messianic testimonials of Isaiah. All of this profound legacy of truth confirms gospel verities and stirs the heart to greater valor in following the principles of the Plan of Salvation as empowered by the Savior's atoning sacrifice.

This modest anthology is intended to render more convenient a daily excursion into the vaults of wisdom preserved for our spiritual nourishment in the Old Testament. Each scriptural passage is paired with a relevant quotation and a listing of additional recommended passages of scripture dealing with the theme of the day. The volume concludes with a cross-referenced thematic index to assist the student of the scriptures to find desired topics contained in this collection.

The compilers of this volume express the hope that these pages may be a useful adjunct study resource for strengthening testimonies and increasing faith.

Ed J. Pinegar
Richard J. Allen

JANUARY

*And in that day Adam blessed God
and was filled, and began
to prophesy . . .*

—MOSES 5:10

JANUARY 1
Come to Know God

And he Moses saw God face to face, and he talked with him, and the glory of God was upon Moses; therefore Moses could endure his presence.

And God spake unto Moses, saying: Behold, I am the Lord God Almighty, and Endless is my name; for I am without beginning of days or end of years; and is not this endless?

And, behold, thou art my son; wherefore look, and I will show thee the workmanship of mine hands.

MOSES 1:2-4

See also John 17:3; D&C 67:10; Moses 1:11.

But few understand the character of God. They do not know, they do not understand their relationship to God. . . . What kind of a being is God? . . . This is a question that may occupy your attention. The scriptures inform us that this is eternal life, to know the only wise God and Jesus Christ whom he has sent. . . .Go back and find out what kind of being God is.

(Kent P. Jackson, comp. and ed., *Joseph Smith's Commentary on the Bible* [Salt Lake City: Deseret Book, 1994], 141.)

JANUARY 2
Be Not Deceived—Call upon God

And again Moses said: I will not cease to call upon God, I have other things to inquire of him: for his glory has been upon me, wherefore I can judge between him and thee.

MOSES 1:18

See also Gen. 12:8; Dan. 6:10; Joel 2:32; Moses 5:8.

Prayer and study must be used together to build knowledge and wisdom.

First, we start with the intelligence with which we were born. To our intelligence we add knowledge as we search for answers, study, and educate ourselves. To our knowledge we add experience, which should lead us to a level of wisdom. In addition to our wisdom, we add the help of the Holy Ghost through our prayers of faith, asking for spiritual guidance and strength. Then, and only then, do we reach an understanding in our hearts.

(Robert D. Hales, "Making Righteous Choices at the Crossroads of Life," *Ensign,* Nov. 1988, 10.)

JANUARY 3
All Things Done through the Son of God

Thus saith the Lord, thy redeemer, and he that formed thee from the womb, I am the Lord that maketh all things; that stretcheth forth the heavens alone; that spreadeth abroad the earth by myself.

ISAIAH 44:24

See also 2 Kgs. 19:15; Alma 26:11–12; Moses 1:32–33.

Our Creator and our Redeemer is also our teacher. He taught us how to live. He gave us commandments, and if we follow them, we will receive blessings and happiness in this world and eternal life in the world to come.

And so we see that He whom we should always remember is He who gave us mortal life, He who showed us the way to a happy life, and He who redeems us so we can have immortality and eternal life.

If we keep our covenant that we will always remember him, we can always have his Spirit to be with us. That Spirit will testify of him, and it will guide us into truth.

(Dallin H. Oaks, "Always Remember Him," *Ensign*, May 1988, 30.)

JANUARY 4
The Work and Glory of God

For behold, this is my work and my glory—to
bring to pass the immortality and eternal life of man.

MOSES 1:39

See also 2 Ne. 33:4; D&C 14:7; 75:5.

I thank him and love him for the light and
understanding he brought to the world concerning
the purpose of life—that mortality is a step in an
eternal journey, that we lived before we came here,
that there was design in our coming, that we are
sons and daughters of God our Eternal Father with a
divine and wonderful birthright, that we are here to
be tested and to grow, that, as one man has said, "Life
is a mission and not a career," that death is a step
across the threshold into another realm as real and
as purposeful as this. Infinite is our opportunity to
grow toward Godhood under the plan of our Eternal
Father and His Beloved Son.

(Gordon B. Hinckley, *Teachings of Gordon B. Hinckley* [Salt
Lake City: Deseret Book, 1997], 452.)

JANUARY 5
The Beauty and Grandeur of the Creation

And God saw every thing that he had made, and, behold, it was very good.

GENESIS 1:31

See also Jacob 4:8–9; D&C 76:24.

Nature is the result of divine creation. The beauty therein was planned and organized by one who truly knew beauty. It stands there waiting for us to realize it as a source of joy. . . .You have felt the rain—fresh, clean, life-giving rain. You have watched the stars—bright, shining, and steadfast in the sky. You have seen the grandeur of the mountains as they loom in the background. Imagine Emerald Lake at the foot of Timpanogos glacier as it breathes forth whispers of cool water! . . . If only we could hear these elements! What rich memories and experiences they could tell us of. But we have to take the time—we have to pay the price.

(Rick Ball, *BYU Speeches of the Year,* 1962, 5.)

JANUARY 6
The Word of God Will Come Forth

Now go, write it before them in a table, and note it in a book, that it may be for the time to come for ever and ever.

ISAIAH 30:8

See also Deut. 8:3; 2 Ne. 3:11–12, 19–21; Moses 1:41.

The return of such truths to the earth features simplicity. The faithful Book of Mormon peoples' straightforward "cry from the dust . . . after many generations . . . shall go, even according to the *simpleness of their words. Because of their faith their words* shall proceed forth . . . unto . . . the fruit of thy loins; and the *weakness* of *their words will I make strong in their [posterity's] faith,* unto the remembering of my covenant."

(Neal A. Maxwell, *But for a Small Moment* [Salt Lake City: Bookcraft, 1986], 24.)

JANUARY 7
Pray for Strength

I will go in the strength of the Lord God: I will make mention of thy righteousness, even of thine only.

PSALM 71:16

See also 2 Sam. 22:33; 1 Ne. 7:17; Alma 14:26, Moses 1:20.

Similar testimony of the power of prayer is borne by *President Gordon B. Hinckley*. When sustained in 1961 as a member of the Quorum of the Twelve, he made these remarks: "I am subdued by the confidence of the Lord's Prophet in me, and by the expressed love of these, my brethren, beside whom I feel like a pygmy. I pray for strength; I pray for help; and I pray for the faith and the will to be obedient. I think that I need—and I feel that all of us need—discipline, if this great work is to roll forward as it is ordained to do."

(Russell M. Nelson, *The Power within Us* [Salt Lake City: Deseret Book, 1988], 150.)

JANUARY 8
Foreordination

And God saw these souls that they were good, and he stood in the midst of them, and he said: These I will make my rulers; for he stood among those that were spirits, and he saw that they were good; and he said unto me: Abraham, thou art one of them; thou wast chosen before thou wast born.

ABRAHAM 3:23

See also Jer.1:5; 1 Pet. 1:2, 20; Alma 13:3–9.

Every man who has a calling to minister to the inhabitants of the world was ordained to that very purpose in the Grand Council of heaven before this world was. I suppose I was ordained to this very office in that Grand Council. It is the testimony that I want that I am God's servant, and this people His people. The ancient prophets declared that in the last days the God of heaven should set up a kingdom which should never be destroyed, nor left to other people; and the very time that was calculated on, this people were struggling to bring it out.

(Joseph Smith, *Teachings of the Prophet Joseph Smith,* [Salt Lake City: Deseret Book, 1976], 365.)

JANUARY 9
Talk with God through Prayer

The Lord is far from the wicked: but he heareth the prayer of the righteous.

PROVERBS 15:29

See also Gen. 4:26; Matt. 26:41; Mosiah 4:11; Abr. 3:11.

When we use these sacred words, "in the name of Jesus Christ," . . . [w]e are on holy ground, brothers and sisters. We are using a name most sublime, most holy, and most wonderful—the very name of the Son of God. We are now able to come unto the Father through His Beloved Son. What power and reassurance and peace come when we really pray in His name. This conclusion to the prayer may, in many ways, be the most important part of the prayer. We can appeal to the Father through His victorious Son with confidence that our prayers will be heard. We can ask and receive, we can seek and find and subsequently find the open door.

(L. Edward Brown, "Pray unto the Father in My Name," *Ensign,* May 1997, 79.)

JANUARY 10
Revealing the Will of God to Man

But there is a God in heaven that revealeth secrets, and maketh known to the king Nebuchadnezzar what shall be in the latter days. Thy dream, and the visions of thy head upon thy bed, are these.

DANIEL 2:28

See also Amos 3:7; D&C 68:3–7; 89:2; Abr. 3:15; A of F 1:9.

All true doctrine will have revelation as its source. It will come from the Father in the name of Christ. It must be taught and learned by the Spirit of revelation. True doctrine will always declare God and revelation as its source. It will never be based upon "philosophical speculation."

(Joseph Fielding McConkie, *Answers: Straightforward Answers to Tough Gospel Questions* [Salt Lake City: Deseret Book, 1998], 217.)

JANUARY 11
Life Is a Test

And we will prove them herewith, to see if they will do all things whatsoever the Lord their God shall command them.

Abraham 3:25

See also Deut. 6:1; 2 Ne. 2:11, 21, 27; Alma 12:24.

The restored gospel of Jesus Christ gives us help in knowing how to qualify for the strength of the Lord as we deal with adversity. It tells us why we face tests in life. And, even more importantly, it tells us how to get protection and help from the Lord.

We have trials to face because our Heavenly Father loves us. His purpose is to help us qualify for the blessing of living with Him and His Son, Jesus Christ, forever in glory and in families. To qualify for that gift we had to receive a mortal body. With that mortality we understood that we would be tested by temptations and by difficulties.

(Henry B. Eyring, "In the Strength of the Lord," *Ensign,* May 2004, 16.)

JANUARY 12

Keeping Our Second Estate

And they who keep their first estate shall be added upon; and they who keep not their first estate shall not have glory in the same kingdom with those who keep their first estate; and they who keep their second estate shall have glory added upon their heads for ever and ever.

ABRAHAM 3:26

See also Gen. 1:28; 1 Cor. 15:58; 2 Ne. 31:20; D&C 6:13.

And what does it mean to keep your second estate? It means to subscribe to all of the laws of the gospel of the Son of God. That is what it means to keep your second estate, to make your calling and election sure. And they who keep their second estate shall have glory added upon their heads forever and forever.

(Bryant S. Hinckley, *Sermons and Missionary Services of Melvin J. Ballard* [Salt Lake City: Deseret Book, 1949], 224.)

JANUARY 13
Do the Will of God

I delight to do thy will, O my God: yea, thy law is within my heart.

PSALM 40:8

See also Josh. 24:14; Luke 22:42; D&C 88:67; Moses 4:2.

It is for me to do the will of God today, and when tomorrow comes, to inquire what is his will concerning me; then do the will of my Father in the work he has appointed me to do, and that is enough for me. I am serving a God who will give me all I merit, when I come to receive my reward. This is what I have always thought; and if I still think so, it is enough for me.

(Brigham Young, *Discourses of Brigham Young* [Salt Lake City: Deseret Book, 1954], 12–13.)

JANUARY 14
The Reality of Satan

Now there was a day when the sons of God came to present themselves before the Lord, and Satan came also among them.

JOB 1:6

See also Isa. 14:12–15; Luke 22:31; Moses 4:4; 5:13.

The devil is a real person with a real power that is the counterfeit or opposite of good. This is the power of evil. The devil is an enemy of God. He seeks the misery of all mankind. He has the ability to tempt people who have reached the age of accountability if they let him. The Book of Mormon calls this "listing" to obey him. Christ is the power we need to reject Satan. That is, if we exercise the will to live righteously and seek his help, Christ will give us his spirit and power.

(Glenn L. Pearson and Reid E. Bankhead, *Building Faith with the Book of Mormon* [Salt Lake City: Bookcraft, 1986], 46.)

JANUARY 15
Jesus Christ as Creator

I have made the earth, and created man upon it:
I, even my hands, have stretched out the heavens, and
all their host have I commanded.

ISAIAH 45:12

See also Gen. 1:26; John 1:1–4; Eph. 3:9; Moses 1:32–33.

The Prophet Joseph Smith and Sidney Rigdon
declared that 'the worlds are and were created' by
Jesus Christ. . . . The following graphically describes
the number of these worlds created by Christ: "Worlds
without number! Innumerable unto man! . . . Count
the grains of sand on all seashores and Saharas of
the world, add the stars in the firmament for good
measure, multiply the total by like sums from other
worlds, and what do we have? Scarcely a dot in the
broad expanse of an infinite universe—all created by
Christ."

(Hoyt W. Brewster, Jr., *Doctrine and Covenants Encyclopedia*
[Salt Lake City: Bookcraft, 1988], 650.)

JANUARY 16
One Eternal Round

But only an account of this earth, and the inhabitants thereof, give I unto you. For behold, there are many worlds that have passed away by the word of my power. And there are many that now stand, and innumerable are they unto man; but all things are numbered unto me, for they are mine and I know them.

MOSES 1:35
See also Isa. 45:18; Moses 1:33–34.

Those who try to qualify God's omniscience fail to understand that He has no need to avoid ennui by learning new things. Because God's love is also perfect, there is, in fact, divine delight in that "one eternal round" which, to us, seems to be all routine and repetition. God derives His great and continuing joy and glory by increasing and advancing His creations, and not from new intellectual experiences.

(Neal A. Maxwell, *All These Things Shall Give Thee Experience* [Salt Lake City: Deseret Book, 1979], 14–15.)

JANUARY 17
Created in the Image of God

And God said, Let us make man in our image, after our likeness: and let them have dominion over the fish of the sea, and over the fowl of the air, and over the cattle, and over all the earth, and over every creeping thing that creepeth upon the earth.

GENESIS 1:26

See also Mosiah 7:27; Moses 2:26–27; Abr. 4:26.

I believe that every brilliant conquest made by man is but a manifestation of the divine spark which sets him apart from the rest of creation. Man is in the image of God, destined to go on learning and perfecting himself throughout eternity. To accept the idea that the human personality ends with death is to accept life as a futile, meaningless gesture.

(Mark E. Petersen, *Adam: Who Is He?* [Salt Lake City: Deseret Book, 1976], 42.)

JANUARY 18
The Joy of Family

And I, God, blessed them, and said unto them: Be fruitful, and multiply, and replenish the earth, and subdue it, and have dominion over the fish of the sea, and over the fowl of the air, and over every living thing that moveth upon the earth.

MOSES 2:28

See also Gen. 1:28; 9:1; Abr. 4:28.

We can hear a voice of gladness that brings exclamations of hope and joy into our lives. The joy of our testimonies of the Savior can punctuate every aspect of our lives as we seek to come unto Christ. . . . It is this light, the light of the restored gospel—a "voice of gladness"—that parents can help their children come to know. The adversary is real, but children can feel the peace and the joy that come as they exercise faith in Jesus Christ. Our children will not experience this light unless we teach them the gospel. . . . We help tune their ears, minds, and hearts to recognize "a voice of gladness" and desire to be worthy to obtain eternal joy when we teach the truths of the gospel.

(Coleen K. Menlove, "A Voice of Gladness for Our Children," *Ensign,* Nov. 2002, 13.)

JANUARY 19
The Sabbath Is Sanctified and Holy

Keep the sabbath day to sanctify it, as the Lord thy God hath commanded thee.

DEUTERONOMY 5:12

See also Gen. 2:3; Ex. 31:13; Mosiah 13:16; Moses 3:3.

The Sabbath is a holy day in which to do worthy and holy things. Abstinence from work and recreation is important but insufficient. The Sabbath calls for constructive thoughts and acts, and if one merely lounges about doing nothing on the Sabbath, he is breaking it. To observe it, one will be on his knees in prayer, preparing lessons, studying the gospel, meditating, visiting the ill and distressed, sleeping, reading wholesome material, and attending all the meetings of that day to which he is expected. To fail to do these proper things is a transgression on the omission side.

(Spencer W. Kimball, *The Miracle of Forgiveness* [Salt Lake City: Bookcraft, 1969], 96–97.)

JANUARY 20

All Things Created Spiritually First

And every plant of the field before it was in the earth, and every herb of the field before it grew. For I, the Lord God, created all things, of which I have spoken, spiritually, before they were naturally upon the face of the earth.

MOSES 3:5

See also JST, Gen. 2:5, 8–10; D&C 29:32; Moses 3:7, 9

As to the character of this spiritual creation nothing is known; nothing, so far as I know, has been revealed in relation to it. Here let me say, by way of caution, that those who accept the revelations of God as truth need not be alarmed if they meet with things in the sacred writings that they cannot explain or understand, as in the case of this spiritual creation of the heavens and the earth which preceded the natural, or what we regard as the actual creation of the earth.

(B. H. Roberts, *The Gospel and Man's Relationship to Deity* [Salt Lake City: Deseret News, 1901], 266.)

JANUARY 21
Marriage Ordained of God

And the Lord God said, It is not good that the man should be alone; I will make him an help meet for him.

GENESIS 2:18

See also Gen. 2:24; Matt 19:5; 1 Cor. 11:11; Moses 3:18.

No man can be saved and exalted in the kingdom of God without the woman, and no woman can reach the perfection and exaltation in the kingdom of God alone. . . . God instituted marriage in the beginning. . . . It was designed that they should be united together in sacred bonds of marriage, and one is not perfect without the other. Furthermore, it means that there is no union for time and eternity that can be perfected outside of the law of God, and the order of his house.

(Joseph F. Smith, *Gospel Doctrine: Selections from the Sermons and Writings of Joseph F. Smith* [Salt Lake City: Deseret Book, 1939], 272.)

JANUARY 22
Beguiled by the Devil

And the Lord God said unto the woman, What is this that thou hast done? And the woman said, The serpent beguiled me, and I did eat.

GENESIS 3:13

See also 2 Ne. 9:9; Ether 8:25.

It is easy enough to see how a world willingly beguiled by the devil's dialectic is bound to reject God's way and continue with its own. Even the Saints are guilty: "Repent, repent, is the voice of God to Zion: and strange as it may appear, yet it is true, mankind will persist in *self-justification* until all their iniquity is exposed, and their character past being redeemed" (pp.18–19, italics added). As in every other dispensation, the world will continue to go its way, which is one of *progressive deterioration.*

(Hugh Nibley, "Beyond Politics," *BYU Studies*, vol. 15 (1974–1975), 13.)

JANUARY 23
Enmity between Mankind and Satan

And I will put enmity between thee and the woman, and between thy seed and her seed; it shall bruise thy head, and thou shalt bruise his heel.

GENESIS 3:15

See also Rom. 8:7; James 4:4; D&C 101:26; Moses 4:21.

The Lord has placed enmity between mortals and Satan. However, individuals can lose this fear of the archenemy if they follow his encouragements and temptations. Before they know it, they become all too familiar with Satan as they come under his bonds and buffetings. However, the righteous maintain a distrust and hostility toward the devil and never become familiar with him. Their enmity toward him along with the Lord's protection guarantees that he will never have power to tempt them beyond their means to withstand.

(Victor L. Ludlow, *Unlocking the Old Testament* [Salt Lake City: Deseret Book, 1981], 8.)

JANUARY 24
The Word of God Will Always Be Fulfilled

For as I, the Lord God, liveth, even so my words cannot return void, for as they go forth out of my mouth they must be fulfilled.

Moses 4:30

See also Amos 3:7; Alma 3:14; D&C 1:38; 21:4–6; 101:64.

I say it in humility, and with full confidence that the word of God shall be fulfilled, and the Church of Jesus Christ of Latter-day Saints shall continue and abide, and the gospel it brings shall be preached to the living and to the dead, until all of the race of Adam, who are able to receive and hear, shall hear the word and have the free opportunity and liberty, if they will, to obey it.

(Charles W. Penrose, *Conference Report*, April 1920, 27.)

And he gave unto them commandments, that they should worship the Lord their God, and should offer the firstlings of their flocks, for an offering unto the Lord. And Adam was obedient unto the commandments of the Lord.

Moses 5:5

See also Gen. 6:22; 22:18; 1 Sam. 15:22; John 14:15.

I give you my testimony that the happiness of the Latter-day Saints, the peace of the Latter-day Saints, the progress of the Latter-day Saints, the prosperity of the Latter-day Saints, and the eternal salvation and exaltation of this people lie in walking in obedience to the counsels of the priesthood of God.

(Gordon B. Hinckley, *Teachings of Gordon B. Hinckley* [Salt Lake City: Deseret Book, 1997], 401.)

JANUARY 26
Results of the Fall

And Eve, his wife, heard all these things and was glad, saying: Were it not for our transgression we never should have had seed, and never should have known good and evil, and the joy of our redemption, and the eternal life which God giveth unto all the obedient.

MOSES 5:11

See also Gen. 2:17; 3:6–7; 2 Ne. 2:19–25; Alma 34:9.

It was Eve who first transgressed the limits of Eden in order to initiate the conditions of mortality. Her act, whatever its nature, was formally a transgression but eternally a glorious necessity to open the doorway toward eternal life. Adam showed his wisdom by doing the same. And thus Eve and "Adam fell that men might be." . . .

Modern revelation shows that our first parents understood the necessity of the Fall. Adam declared, "Blessed be the name of God, for because of my transgression my eyes are opened, and in this life I shall have joy, and again in the flesh I shall see God."

(Dallin H. Oaks, "The Great Plan of Happiness," *Ensign*, Nov. 1993, 72.)

JANUARY 27
Consequences of Following Satan

And Satan came among them, saying: I am also a son of God; and he commanded them, saying: Believe it not; and they believed it not, and they loved Satan more than God. And men began from that time forth to be carnal, sensual, and devilish.

MOSES 5:13

See also 1 Chr. 21:1; Rom. 8:6; 2 Ne. 9:39; Mosiah 3:19.

Casting off the natural man and struggling to become a follower of Christ is the disciple's first step. It is delineated by Benjamin with a specificity and intensity that make this sermon one of the greatest on record. . . .

We can begin to sense the specific demands of discipleship in terms of the virtues Benjamin encourages his listeners to develop: meekness, humility, patience, love, spiritual submissiveness.

(Neal A. Maxwell, "King Benjamin's Manual of Discipleship," *Ensign*, Jan. 1992, 10.)

JANUARY 28
Repent and Be Saved

For I will declare mine iniquity; I will be sorry for my sin.

Psalm 38:18

See also Num. 5:7; Ps. 51:10; Ezra 10:11; Moses 5:15; 6:57.

When men truly and heartily repent, and make manifest to the heavens that their repentance is genuine by obedience to the requirements made known to them through the laws of the Gospel, then are they entitled to the administration of salvation, and no power can withhold the good spirit from them.

(Brigham Young, *Discourses of Brigham Young* [Salt Lake City: Deseret Book, 1954], 156.)

JANUARY 29
Blessings of the Gospel Principles

And he also said unto him: If thou wilt turn unto me, and hearken unto my voice, and believe, and repent of all thy transgressions, and be baptized, even in water, in the name of mine Only Begotten Son, who is full of grace and truth, which is Jesus Christ, the only name which shall be given under heaven, whereby salvation shall come unto the children of men, ye shall receive the gift of the Holy Ghost, asking all things in his name, and whatsoever ye shall ask, it shall be given you.

MOSES 6:52

See also Job 19:25–27; Isa. 55:7; 3 Ne. 9:20; 27:13–22.

The First Presidency of the Church has said that all of the ordinances of the Gospel pertain to the celestial kingdom of God. . . . President Brigham Young . . . informed the Elders . . . to bring people to repentance and into the celestial kingdom of God, and that is our mission and responsibility to the people of the earth.

(Joseph Fielding Smith, *Church History and Modern Revelation* [Salt Lake City: The Church of Jesus Christ of Latter-day Saints, 1946–1949], 2:60–61.)

JANUARY 30
Teach Your Children the Plan of Salvation

Wherefore teach it unto your children, that all men, everywhere, must repent, or they can in nowise inherit the kingdom of God . . . Therefore I give unto you a commandment, to teach these things freely unto your children, saying . . . ye must be born again into the kingdom of heaven, of water, and of the Spirit, and be cleansed by blood, even the blood of mine Only Begotten; that ye might be sanctified from all sin, and enjoy the words of eternal life in this world, and eternal life in the world to come, even immortal glory.

MOSES 6:57–59

See also Gen. 18:19; Deut. 4:9; Prov. 22:6; Enos 1:1.

Teach your little children while they are at your knee and they will grow up to be stalwart. They may stray away, but your love and your faith will bring them back.

(Harold B. Lee, *The Teachings of Harold B. Lee* [Salt Lake City: Bookcraft, 1996], 273.)

JANUARY 31
Justification and Sanctification

In the Lord shall all the seed of Israel be justified, and shall glory.

ISAIAH 45:25

See also Isa. 13:12; 53:11; Ezek. 37:28; Moses 6:60.

The gift of grace or mercy is received as a believer repents, enters into the specified covenants, and receives the Holy Ghost. This action of acceptance on our part opens the door for the process of justification (remission, or pardoning, of sins) and sanctification (cleansing from sin) to work in us—something we may refer to as being born again . . . Justification and sanctification are accomplished by the grace of Christ, which grace is a gift to man based on faith. But our moral agency is also a necessary element in this divine process. We must will to repent and act to repent. We must elect to be baptized and receive the Holy Ghost, and we must elect to remain loyal to our covenants thereafter. To receive the gift we must act in the manner He has ordained.

(D. Todd Christofferson, "Justification and Sanctification," *Ensign,* June 2001, 23–24.)

EBRUARY

*And Elijah came unto all the people,
and said, How long halt ye between
atwo opinions? if the Lord be God,
bfollow him: but if Baal, then follow
him. And the people answered him not
a word.*

—1 KINGS 18:21

FEBRUARY 1
Blessings of the Holy Ghost

Therefore it is given to abide in you; the record of heaven; the Comforter; the peaceable things of immortal glory; the truth of all things; that which quickeneth all things, which maketh alive all things; that which knoweth all things, and hath all power according to wisdom, mercy, truth, justice, and judgment.

MOSES 6:61

See also Ex. 31:3; 1 Sam. 10:6; John 15:26; Moro. 8:26.

People who have "an eye of faith" and who have "the law written in their hearts" will not only enjoy the companionship of the Holy Spirit but also will receive special blessings and promises.

(Carlos E. Asay, *The Road to Somewhere: A Guide for Young Men and Women* [Salt Lake City: Bookcraft, 1994], 13.)

FEBRUARY 2
Gospel Preached since the Beginning

And thus the Gospel began to be preached, from the beginning, being declared by holy angels sent forth from the presence of God, and by his own voice, and by the gift of the Holy Ghost.

And thus all things were confirmed unto Adam, by an holy ordinance, and the Gospel preached, and a decree sent forth, that it should be in the world, until the end thereof; and thus it was.

MOSES 5:58–59

See also Isa. 40:9; 52:7; 61:1; Matt. 28:19.

It must be remembered that this Church has a great mission and a great responsibility: to preach the Gospel in all the nations . . . to advance the work of salvation for the dead,—and to promote the temporal as well as the spiritual welfare of its members. All these things require much means as well as voluntary service. Every member of the Church is expected to do his or her part to help in these various respects.

(Sylvester Q. Cannon, *Conference Report*, October 1935, 112.)

FEBRUARY 3
Record Keeping—A Commandment

❧

And Moses wrote all the words of the Lord, and
rose up early in the morning, and builded an altar
under the hill, and twelve pillars, according to the
twelve tribes of Israel.

EXODUS 24:4

See also Rev. 1:19; 2 Ne. 5:29; D&C 21:1; 85:1; Moses 6:5.

If the commandment to keep records had not
been given, and no records had been kept regarding
the dealings of the Lord with mankind, this world
would have dwindled into savagery, and Satan would
have taken it completely captive. There would have
been no knowledge pertaining to earlier generations.
The Lord in his mercy and love saw to it that his
word was recorded, and though much of it has come
down to us in corrupted form, nevertheless, by the
power of the Almighty much has been preserved. It
is upon divine records that nations have based their
civilizations to a marked degree.

(Joseph Fielding Smith, *Answers to Gospel Questions* [Salt
Lake City: Deseret Book, 1957–1966], 2:71.)

FEBRUARY 4
Power of Faith

And he believed in the Lord; and he counted it to him for righteousness.

GENESIS 15:6

See also Dan. 6:23; Hab. 2:4; Alma 14:26; Moses 7:13.

Jesus recognized this wonderfully creative, dynamic power of faith. He likened it unto a mustard seed and said that he who had faith even as a grain of mustard seed could move mountains; that nothing would be impossible to him. Faith is like a seed because of its great potential to multiply itself, to increase reality.

(Lowell L. Bennion, *The Best of Lowell L. Bennion: Selected Writings 1928–1988* [Salt Lake City: Deseret Book, 1988], 182.)

FEBRUARY 5
A Zion People

And the Lord called his people ZION, because they were of one heart and one mind, and dwelt in righteousness; and there was no poor among them.

MOSES 7:18

See also Gen. 5:24; D&C 6:6; 97:21; 105:5.

Over many years he [Enoch] continued to preach righteousness and built a city—the "City of Holiness—even Zion," and the Lord called this people Zion. . . . Enoch's people came to be of one heart, one mind; they dwelt in righteousness and there were no poor among them, and the glory of the Lord was upon His people. Zion, in process of time (365 years), was taken up into God's own bosom. The saying then went forth, "Zion is fled."

(Neal A. Maxwell, *Of One Heart/Look Back at Sodom* [Salt Lake City: Deseret Book, 1990], 64.)

FEBRUARY 6
The Latter Days

And truth will I send forth out of the earth, to bear testimony of mine Only Begotten; . . . gather out mine elect from the four quarters of the earth, unto a place which I shall prepare, an Holy City, that my people may gird up their loins, and be looking forth for the time of my coming; for there shall be my tabernacle, and it shall be called Zion, a New Jerusalem.

MOSES 7:62

See also Gen. 49:22; Ps. 85:11; Isa. 29; D&C 84:2.

We stand on the brink of the next century. From this vantage point, we need to remember that the most significant events in the last 2,000 years were not the marvels of science, technology, and travel. They were the Savior's Atonement and the restoration of the gospel, with the priesthood keys and authority. These two singular events will continue to be of transcendent importance to mankind as we move forward in time. The past, present, and future pivot on these marvelous divine interventions.

(James E. Faust, "This Is Our Day," *Ensign,* May 1999, 17.)

FEBRUARY 7
Declare the Gospel of Jesus Christ

And in very deed for this cause have I raised thee up, for to shew in thee my power; and that my name may be declared throughout all the earth.

Exodus 9:16

See also Isa. 61:1; Jonah 3:2; 1 Cor. 9:16; Moses 8:19.

The Prophet was instructed to tell him [Oliver Cowdery] to continue in bearing witness before the world, and he was not supposed to think he could say enough in the Lord's cause. . . . At all times and in all places he was to open his mouth and declare the Gospel as with the voice of a trump, both day and night and in this the Lord would give him strength such as is not known among men.

(Joseph Fielding Smith, *Church History and Modern Revelation* [Salt Lake City: The Church of Jesus Christ of Latter-day Saints, 1946–1949], 1:114–115.)

FEBRUARY 8
Repent or Perish

He that covereth his sins shall not prosper: but whoso confesseth and forsaketh them shall have mercy.

PROVERBS 28:13

See also Neh. 9:2; Ezek. 18:21; Alma 9:12; Moses 8:20.

Repentance is not optional. An angel commanded Adam to "repent and call upon God in the name of the Son forevermore." Each one of us is commanded to both repent and to call upon God continually throughout life. That pattern allows each day to be an unspoiled page in the book of life, a new, fresh opportunity. We are given the rejuvenating privilege of overcoming mistakes of commission or omission, be they small or profoundly serious. Full repentance results in forgiveness with spiritual renewal. One can feel the cleansing, the purity, the freshness that accompanies sincere repentance at any time in life.

(Richard G. Scott, "The Path to Peace and Joy," *Ensign*, Nov. 2000, 25.)

FEBRUARY 9
Wicked Are Destroyed

Ye have plowed wickedness, ye have reaped iniquity; ye have eaten the fruit of lies: because thou didst trust in thy way, in the multitude of thy mighty men.

HOSEA 10:13

See also Gen. 6:17; Moses 8:26, 30.

The people before the flood, and also the Sodomites and Canaanites, had carried these corruptions and degeneracies so far that God, in mercy, destroyed them and thus put an end to the procreation of races so degenerate and abominable; while Noah, Abraham, Melchizedek, and others who were taught in the true laws of procreation "were perfect in their generation," and trained their children in the same laws.

(Parley P. Pratt, *Key to the Science of Theology,* in H. Donl Peterson, *The Pearl of Great Price: A History and Commentary* [Salt Lake City: Deseret Book, 1987], 230.)

FEBRUARY 10

Obedience to the Commandments of God

Thus did Noah; according to all that God commanded him, so did he.

GENESIS 6:22

See also Gen. 26:5; Ex. 24:7; Deut. 30:20; Jer. 7:23.

I am so grateful for God's gift of laws and commandments. Peace, hope, and direction are outcomes of striving to live the teachings of Jesus and obeying His laws and commandments. The scriptures teach, "Great peace have they which love thy law." They also teach that "he who doeth the works of righteousness shall receive his reward, even peace in this world, and eternal life in the world to come."

(Patricia P. Pinegar, "Peace, Hope, and Direction," *Ensign,* Nov. 1999, 67.)

FEBRUARY 11
Consequences for Not Hearkening to the Lord

The way of a fool is right in his own eyes: but he that hearkeneth unto counsel is wise.

PROVERBS 12:15

See also Deut. 11:28; 2 Kgs. 18:12; Jer. 9:13–16.

It is frequently said that order is the first law of heaven. I wish to put this in a different light. Order in the Church is the result of obedience to the laws of God and to the discipline which He has established among men. . . . Without obedience there can be no order, no discipline, no government. The will of God cannot be done, either in the heavens or on the earth, except men will obey the will of the Father. And when men obey the will of the Father, order is the result.

(Joseph F. Smith, in Brian H. Stuy, ed., *Collected Discourses* [Burbank, CA, and Woodland Hills, UT: B.H.S., 1987–1992], 5.)

FEBRUARY 12
Seek Righteousness

And, finding there was greater happiness and peace and rest for me, I sought for the blessings of the fathers, and the right whereunto I should be ordained to administer the same; having been myself a follower of righteousness, desiring also to be one who possessed great knowledge, and to be a greater follower of righteousness, and to possess a greater knowledge, and to be a father of many nations, a prince of peace, and desiring to receive instructions, and to keep the commandments of God, I became a rightful heir, a High Priest, holding the right belonging to the fathers.

ABRAHAM 1:2

See also Prov. 11:18; Zeph. 2:3; Acts 10:35; D&C 20:14.

The missionaries find ample compensation for the great work they are doing when they see honest souls who seek after righteousness brought to a knowledge of the truth through their instrumentality.

(LeGrand Richards, *Conference Report,* October 1958, 111.)

FEBRUARY 13
Pray Always

Then shall ye call upon me, and ye shall go and pray unto me, and I will hearken unto you.

And ye shall seek me, and find me, when ye shall search for me with all your heart.

JEREMIAH 29:12–13

See also 2 Chr. 7:14; 2 Ne. 32:9; 3 Ne. 18:18; D&C 10:5.

After the injunction to pray in families, Christ taught that we should meet in church "oft" and should pray for all who seek the Church, forbidding or casting out none. As this discourse concludes, it is clear and unequivocal that the "light" we are to hold up to the world is the fact that we pray—and pray always—as Christ prayed unto the Father.

(Jeffrey R. Holland, *Christ and the New Covenant: The Messianic Message of the Book of Mormon* [Salt Lake City: Deseret Book, 1997], 273.)

FEBRUARY 14
The Abrahamic Covenant

And I will make of thee a great nation . . . and
thou shalt be a blessing unto thy seed after thee,
that in their hands they shall bear this ministry
and Priesthood unto all nations; . . . . and shall be
accounted thy seed, and shall rise up and bless thee,
as their father . . . for I give unto thee a promise that
this right shall continue in thee, and in thy seed after
thee . . . shall all the families of the earth be blessed,
even with the blessings of the Gospel, which are the
blessings of salvation, even of life eternal.

ABRAHAM 2:9–11

See also Gen. 12:3; 18:18,19; 26:4; 2 Ne. 29:14.

Abraham received the covenant and lived worthy
of its consummate privileges, even exaltation and
godhood—because of these things we have come to
call the covenant which God makes with his people
the Abrahamic covenant.

(Joseph Fielding McConkie and Robert L. Millet, *Doctrinal
Commentary on the Book of Mormon* [Salt Lake City: Bookcraft,
1987–1992], 4:143.)

FEBRUARY 15
Covenant Making

Gather my saints together unto me; those that have made a covenant with me by sacrifice.

PSALM 50:5

See also Gen. 9:15; 2 Chr. 34:31.

Knowing and remembering who we are and whose we are, we become guided by a force affecting our attitude and our conduct. We draw close to our Father in Heaven through sacred ordinances and covenants available only through His restored church. . . . It is our faith in the importance of making covenants with God and coming to understand our immense possibilities that the temple, the house of the Lord, becomes the focus for all that really matters. In the temple we participate in ordinances and covenants that span the distance between heaven and earth. They prepare us to one day return to God's presence and enjoy the blessings of eternal families and eternal life.

(Ardeth G. Kapp, "A Mighty Force for Righteousness," *Ensign,* May 1992, 79.)

FEBRUARY 16
Remembering Our Covenants

Take heed unto yourselves, lest ye forget the covenant of the Lord your God, which he made with you, and make you a graven image, or the likeness of any thing, which the Lord thy God hath forbidden thee.

DEUTERONOMY 4:23

See also Gen. 17:10; Ex. 19:5; Luke 1:72.

Except we do walk uprightly and remember our covenants and have an unshakable testimony of the divinity of this Church; in the language of an eminent businessman and financier, the various activities of the Church would be but a shambles.

(Harold B. Lee, *Conference Report*, April 1962, 32.)

FEBRUARY 17
Keeping and Honoring Our Covenants

They shall ask the way to Zion with their faces thitherward, saying, Come, and let us join ourselves to the Lord in a perpetual covenant that shall not be forgotten.

JEREMIAH 50:5

See also D&C 136:4.

Anciently the Lord made covenants with His children to help them remember who they were and what was expected of them. . . . In our day, we again have a chance to make covenants to keep us in remembrance that we are sons and daughters of God desiring to return to His presence. . . . Keeping our covenants should make a difference in the way we live, the way we act, the way we speak, the way we dress, the way we treat each other. If we "always remember him," we will "always have his Spirit to be with us." Then with that Spirit we will be viewed by the world as distinct and different in happy ways.

(Joanne B. Doxey, "Remember Him," *Ensign,* Nov. 1989, 91.)

FEBRUARY 18

Make Our Covenants with the Lord

And the king stood by a pillar, and made a covenant before the Lord, to walk after the Lord, and to keep his commandments and his testimonies and his statutes with all their heart and all their soul, to perform the words of this covenant that were written in this book. And all the people stood to the covenant.

2 KINGS 23:3

See also Zech. 9:11; Moro. 4:3; 5:2. D&C 54:6.

How did you feel the last time you partook of the sacrament? Did you ponder those covenants made in fonts and within temples? The sacrament enables us to renew our covenants. Thus, if we keep those covenants with honor and exactness, we can feel as fresh and as pure as we did when we were first baptized. We can feel as committed to a temple sealing as we did as a new bride or groom. . . . Covenants anchor us to solid ground, which, amidst the storms, makes our promises *not only meaningful for eternity but vital for today.*

(Bonnie D. Parkin, "Celebrating Covenants," *Ensign,* May 1995, 78–79.)

FEBRUARY 19
Charity or Contention

And there was a strife between the herdmen of Abram's cattle and the herdmen of Lot's cattle . . . And Abram said unto Lot, Let there be no strife, I pray thee, between me and thee, and between my herdmen and thy herdmen; for we be brethren.

Is not the whole land before thee? separate thyself, I pray thee, from me: if thou wilt take the left hand, then I will go to the right; or if thou depart to the right hand, then I will go to the left.

GENESIS 13:7–9

See also Zech. 7:9; 1 Cor. 13:4.

Contention fosters disunity. The Book of Mormon teaches the better way:

"Alma, having authority from God, . . . commanded them that there should be no contention one with another, but that they should look forward with one eye, having one faith and one baptism, having their hearts knit together in unity and in love one towards another."

(Russell M. Nelson, *Peace* [Salt Lake City: Deseret Book, 1998], 92.)

FEBRUARY 20

Worldliness Will Lead Away from God

Flee out of the midst of Babylon, and deliver every man his soul: be not cut off in her iniquity; for this is the time of the Lord's vengeance; he will render unto her a recompence.

JEREMIAH 51:6

See also Ps. 73:12; James 1:27; Alma 31:27; D&C 1:16.

Gentile influence during the ages of apostasy—whether in the form of Greek philosophy or humanistic theology—had suppressed the truth and driven the Church of God into the wilderness. Worldliness had replaced godliness; philosophy had replaced true religion; rhetoric had replaced prophecy; and reason had supplanted revelation. Inappropriate actions will always follow on the heels of false beliefs; what we believe determines what we do.

(Joseph Fielding McConkie and Robert L. Millet, *Doctrinal Commentary on the Book of Mormon* [Salt Lake City: Bookcraft, 1987–1992], 2:61.)

FEBRUARY 21
Tithes and Offerings

And blessed be the most high God, which hath delivered thine enemies into thy hand. And he gave him tithes of all.

GENESIS 14:20

See also Gen. 28:22; Mal. 3:8; D&C 119:4.

Pay your tithes that you may be worthy of the Lord's blessings . . . as the Lord has promised: "I, the Lord, am bound when ye do what I say; but when ye do not what I say, ye have no promise." The Lord honors His covenants. I am so thankful for the law of tithing. I believe in it with all my heart.

(Gordon B. Hinckley, *Teachings of Gordon B. Hinckley* [Salt Lake City: Deseret Book, 1997], 659.)

FEBRUARY 22

All Things Are Possible with the Lord

Is any thing too hard for the Lord? At the time appointed I will return unto thee, according to the time of life, and Sarah shall have a son.

GENESIS 18:14

See also Job 42:2; Jer. 32:17; Matt. 19:26; 1 Ne. 7:12.

It is time, with the experience we have had now as a Church, that we should be a people of unbounded faith, willing to believe that all things are possible with God and that when He commands us to do anything, we should go to with our might and with unyielding determination to accomplish that end according to the mind and will of God. This is the kind of people God expects us to be.

(George Q. Cannon, *Gospel Truth: Discourses and Writings of President George Q. Cannon* [Salt Lake City: Deseret Book, 1987], 115.)

FEBRUARY 23
All Nations Blessed through Abraham's Seed

And the Lord said, Shall I hide from Abraham that thing which I do;

Seeing that Abraham shall surely become a great and mighty nation, and all the nations of the earth shall be blessed in him?

GENESIS 18:17–18

See also Gen. 12:3; 28:14; 2 Ne. 29:14; D&C 110:12.

In bearing witness of Christ, Paul drew upon the prophetic promise that through Abraham's seed all humanity would be blessed. . . . It is certainly true that all nations would be blessed through Abraham's seed—meaning his endless posterity, through which the blessings of the gospel, the priesthood, and eternal life would be dispensed to the world. However, the ultimate fulfillment of the Abrahamic promise came through the One who was truly the Chosen Seed, Jesus of Nazareth, son of David and thus son of Abraham.

(Robert L. Millet, *Selected Writings of Robert L. Millet: Gospel Scholars Series* [Salt Lake City: Deseret Book, 2000], 80–81.)

FEBRUARY 24
The Lord Will Destroy the Wicked

Then the Lord rained upon Sodom and upon Gomorrah brimstone and fire from the Lord out of heaven;

And he overthrew those cities, and all the plain, and all the inhabitants of the cities, and that which grew upon the ground.

Genesis 19:24–25

See also Prov. 10:7; 1 Ne. 22:15; 2 Ne. 13:11; 23:11,15, 22.

The LDS Bible Dictionary indicates that "conditions of desolation, born of abomination and wickedness, were to occur *twice* in fulfillment of Daniel's words." The first of these was when Jerusalem was destroyed in a.d. 70, and the second is when the city will once again be besieged in the last days. It further states that "in a general sense, abomination of desolation also describes the latter-day judgments to be poured out upon the wicked wherever they may be."

(Hoyt W. Brewster, Jr., *Doctrine and Covenants Encyclopedia* [Salt Lake City: Bookcraft, 1988], 131.)

FEBRUARY 25
The World's Hold upon the Souls of Mankind

But his wife looked back from behind him, and
she became a pillar of salt.

GENESIS 19:26.

See also Gen. 19:14; Luke 17:31–32

The crass condition of the men of Sodom and
the spiritual lassitude of some members of Lot's family
make it evident why mercy must not overrule justice
and permit the wicked to escape the fruits of evil-
doing. The hesitant family of Lot could not justly be
saved without some test of their faith and worthiness.
Some did not accept the warning, and even Lot's wife
looked back in spite of being led out by the hand and
being duly warned. She perished in the holocaust with
the others who refused to heed. Jesus used this lesson
in his prophecy about the end of our wicked world; it
concludes: "Remember Lot's wife."

(Ellis T. Rasmussen, *A Latter-day Saint Commentary on the
Old Testament* [Salt Lake City: Deseret, 1993], 48–49.)

FEBRUARY 26
Beware False Worship

My fathers, having turned from their righteousness, and from the holy commandments which the Lord their God had given unto them, unto the worshiping of the gods of the heathen, utterly refused to hearken to my voice.

ABRAHAM 1:5

See also Ex. 20:3; Isa. 2:8; 2 Ne. 9:37; Alma 17:15.

But how do we follow him if first we don't find him? And how shall we find him if first we don't seek him? Where and how should we begin this search for Jesus? Some have attempted to answer these questions by turning to idols, others by burning incense or lighting candles. In times past, great throngs journeyed in the crusades of Christianity, feeling that if only the Holy Land could be secured from the infidel, then Christ would be found in their lives. How mistaken they were! Thousands upon thousands perished; many others committed heinous crimes in the very name of Christianity. *Jesus will not be found by crusades of men.*

(Thomas S. Monson, *The Search for Jesus* [Salt Lake City: Deseret Book, 1992], 7–8.)

FEBRUARY 27
The Lord Delivers His Servants

And as they lifted up their hands upon me, that they might offer me up and take away my life, behold, I lifted up my voice unto the Lord my God, and the Lord hearkened and heard, and he filled me with the vision of the Almighty, and the angel of his presence stood by me, and immediately unloosed my bands.

ABRAHAM 1:15

See also Ex. 18:9–10; 2 Tim. 3:11; 1 Ne. 7:11; Alma 5:5.

It is also of equal importance that men should have the idea of the existence of the attribute judgment in God, in order that they may exercise faith in him for life and salvation; for without the idea of the existence of this attribute in the Deity, it would be impossible for men to exercise faith in him for life and salvation, seeing that it is through the exercise of this attribute that the faithful in Christ Jesus are delivered out of the hands of those who seek their destruction.

(*Lectures on Faith* 4:14.)

FEBRUARY 28
Offer All to the Lord

And he said, Take now thy son, thine only son Isaac, whom thou lovest, and get thee into the land of Moriah; and offer him there for a burnt offering upon one of the mountains which I will tell thee of.

GENESIS 22:2

See also Gen. 8:20; Ps. 4:5; Matt. 19:21; 3 Ne. 9:20.

We have entered into the bond of that new and everlasting covenant agreeing that we would obey the commandments of God in all things whatsoever he shall command us. This is an everlasting covenant even unto the end of our days. And when is the end of our days? . . . We shall never see the day in time nor in eternity, when it will not be obligatory, and when it will not be a pleasure as well as a duty for us, as his children, to obey all the commandments of the Lord throughout the endless ages of eternity.

(Joseph F. Smith, *Gospel Doctrine: Selections from the Sermons and Writings of Joseph F. Smith* [Salt Lake City: Deseret Book, 1939], 210.)

ARCH

Then Esther the queen answered and
said, If I have found favour in thy
sight, O king, and if it please the king,
let my life be given me at my petition,
and my people at my request.

—ESTHER 7:3

MARCH 1
God Will Provide

❦

And Isaac spake unto Abraham his father, and said, My father: and he said, Here am I, my son. And he said, Behold the fire and the wood: but where is the lamb for a burnt offering?

And Abraham said, My son, God will provide himself a lamb for a burnt offering: so they went both of them together.

Genesis 22:7–8

See also 1 Ne. 3:7; 17:3; Mosiah 7:19; Alma 26:11–12.

It is for us to attend the instructions we receive from those who are called to teach us, and do our duty in the office and calling unto which we are appointed, and Heaven will provide and take care we get those things which we need. . . . We are to provide the wood and fire, and the lamb God will provide in his own due time. Our greatest concern ought to be how to discharge the duties that are made obligatory upon us—how to act in our respective callings with an eye single to the glory of God.

(Orson Hyde, *Journal of Discourses* [London: Latter-day Saints' Book Depot, 1854–1886], 6: 311.)

MARCH 2
Perfect Obedience

And Abraham lifted up his eyes, and looked, and behold behind him a ram caught in a thicket by his horns: and Abraham went and took the ram, and offered him up for a burnt offering in the stead of his son.

GENESIS 22:13

See also Deut. 13:4; Eccl. 12:13; Heb. 12:28; 2 Ne. 1:9.

How exceedingly difficult it must have been for Abraham, in obedience to God's command, to take his beloved Isaac into the land of Moriah, there to present him as a burnt offering. Can you imagine the heaviness of his heart as he gathered the wood for the fire and journeyed to the appointed place? Surely pain must have racked his body and tortured his mind as he "bound Isaac . . . and laid him on the altar upon the wood. And . . . stretched forth his hand, and took the knife to slay his son . . ."

Abraham qualifies as a model of unquestioning obedience.

(Thomas S. Monson, "Models to Follow," *Ensign*, Nov. 2002, 60.)

MARCH 3
Blessings of Obedience

And said, By myself have I sworn, saith the Lord, for because thou hast done this thing, and hast not withheld thy son, thine only son:

That in blessing I will bless thee, and in multiplying I will multiply thy seed as the stars of the heaven, and as the sand which is upon the sea shore; and thy seed shall possess the gate of his enemies;

And in thy seed shall all the nations of the earth be blessed; because thou hast obeyed my voice.

GENESIS 22:16–18

See also Isa. 1:19; Jarom 1:9; Mosiah 2:22.

The benefits and blessings of faith and obedience are everlasting. The products of the Spirit are priceless. Indeed with the blessings of obedience we live closer to God and our neighbor, and appreciate more our earthly heritage in every way. In the words of Peter we are told: "Whereby are given unto us exceeding great and precious promises: that by these ye might be partakers of the divine nature." Thus our obedience to the gospel carries its own reward here and now.

(Henry D. Moyle, *Conference Report,* October 1962, 89.)

MARCH 4
Power and Rights of the Priesthood

Behold, I will lead thee by my hand, and I will take thee, to put upon thee my name, even the Priesthood of thy father, and my power shall be over thee.

As it was with Noah so shall it be with thee; but through thy ministry my name shall be known in the earth forever, for I am thy God.

ABRAHAM 1:18–19

See also Ex. 28:41; Deut. 34:9; D&C 84:21; 107:18–20.

Joseph Smith was the instrument chosen of God and endowed with His authority to restore the holy priesthood, the power of God to bind on earth and in heaven, to loose on earth and in heaven,—the power of the priesthood by which men may perform ordinances of the gospel of Jesus Christ for the salvation of mankind.

(Joseph F. Smith, *Conference Report,* October 1916, 3.)

MARCH 5
Marry in the Covenant

And my master Abraham made me swear, saying, Thou shalt not take a wife to my son Isaac of the daughters of the Canaanites, in whose land I dwell:

But thou shalt go unto my father's house, and to my kindred, and take a wife unto my son.

GENESIS 24:37–38

See also Ezra 10:10; D&C 132:19.

There is nothing we could do, perhaps, that would help our young people to a better realization of their possibilities, than to so teach them that they would marry in the Temple. . . . The very sanctity and sacredness of that thing is one of the greatest supports that we could have in life.

(Antoine R. Ivins, *Conference Report,* April 1941, 31.)

MARCH 6
Covenants and Oaths

And I will make thee swear by the Lord, the God of heaven, and the God of the earth, that thou shalt not take a wife unto my son of the daughters of the Canaanites, among whom I dwell.

GENESIS 24:3

See also Gen. 50:25; Num. 30:2; Mosiah 18:13; D&C 5:3.

Far too many who have been blessed with great ability and exceptional intellect fail to have an "I will" attitude when it comes to going, doing, saying, and being what the Lord commands.

I will go, I will do, I will say, I will be all convey determined obedience. Our third article of faith states, "We believe that through the Atonement of Christ, all mankind may be saved, by obedience to the laws and ordinances of the Gospel." Certainly the most magnificent act of obedience was accomplished in Gethsemane. You may recall the heartfelt plea of the Savior: "Father, if thou be willing, remove this cup from me: nevertheless not my will, but thine, be done."

(H. David Burton, "I Will Go," *Ensign,* Nov. 1995, 43.)

MARCH 7
Preserve Your Divine Heritage

And Esau said, Behold, I am at the point to die: and what profit shall this birthright do to me?

And Jacob said, Swear to me this day; and he sware unto him: and he sold his birthright unto Jacob.

GENESIS 25:32–33

See also Deut. 14:2; Acts 17:29; Rom. 8:16–17.

I pray that we might prepare ourselves, as you here are attempting to do, to become more like that from which we came, being ever conscious of our divine heritage, being ever aware of our royal birth. Let us be loyal to the Royal that is in us.

(Hugh B. Brown, *The Abundant Life* [Salt Lake City: Bookcraft, 1965], 261.)

MARCH 8
The Lord Always Fulfills His Promises

Nevertheless I will remember my covenant with thee in the days of thy youth, and I will establish unto thee an everlasting covenant.

EZEKIEL 16:60

See also Lev. 26:44; Acts 13:23; 2 Ne. 10:17; D&C 1:38.

I rejoice greatly, and praise the Lord, who is our strength, and upon whom we depend for guidance and support, for the manifestation of his goodness to us as it is exemplified in this large assembly of Latter-day Saints who are gathered here for the semi-annual conference of the Church.

As I look upon this congregation and review the circumstances which have brought it together, going back into the remote past, and see, or appear to see, how literally the Lord fulfills his promises to people with whom he enters into covenant, my heart is made to rejoice.

(Anthony W. Ivins, *Conference Report*, October 1926, 13.)

Joys of Eternal Marriage

Live joyfully with the wife whom thou lovest all
the days of the life of thy vanity, which he hath given
thee under the sun, all the days of thy vanity: for that
is thy portion in this life, and in thy labour which
thou takest under the sun.

ECCLESIASTES 9:9

See also Gen. 2:24; Prov. 5:18; 1 Pet. 3:7; 4 Ne. 1:11.

Eternal love, eternal marriage, eternal increase!
This ideal, which is new to many, when thoughtfully
considered, can keep a marriage strong and safe. No
relationship has more potential to exalt a man and a
woman than the marriage covenant. No obligation in
society or in the Church supersedes it in importance.

I thank God for marriage. I thank God for temples. I thank God for the glorious sealing power, that
power which transcends all that we have been given,
through which our marriages may become eternal.
May we be worthy of this sacred gift.

(Boyd K. Packer, "Marriage," *Ensign,* May 1981, 15.)

MARCH 10

Everlasting Covenants

Behold, the days come, saith the Lord, that I will make a new covenant with the house of Israel, and with the house of Judah.

JEREMIAH 31:31

See also Judg. 2:1; 2 Chr. 34:31; Jer. 50:5.

The new and everlasting covenant is the fulness of the gospel of Jesus Christ and embraces every promise and agreement within the divine plan of life and salvation by which the true believer can be admitted into the celestial family of Christ to inherit "all that [the] Father hath."

(William H. Bennett, "Covenants and Blessings," *Ensign,* Nov. 1975, 45.)

MARCH 11
Joy in Righteousness

Thou wilt shew me the path of life: in thy presence is fulness of joy; at thy right hand there are pleasures for evermore.

PSALM 16:11

See also Ps. 97:12; Isa. 29:19.

The dawning of a brighter day heralds a time of forgiveness. Shadows of yesterday's grief melt in the rays of early morning's opportunity. Joy comes from our posterity, and we rejoice as they are blessed by the ordinances of salvation and exaltation.

Our family experienced that in a special way when our youngest daughter was sealed to her eternal companion in the holy temple. There to witness this event, along with other family members, were her parents and all eight of her older sisters and their husbands. For us, there was truly joy in the morning on that day. Then we really felt the scriptural truth, "Men are, that they might have joy."

(Russell M. Nelson, *The Power within Us* [Salt Lake City: Deseret Book, 1988], 81.)

MARCH 12
Growth through Adversity

⟡

If thou faint in the day of adversity, thy strength is small.

PROVERBS 24:10

See also 2 Chr. 15:4; Rom. 5:3–5; D&C 122:7.

In Luke we read of the growth of the Savior from childhood into adulthood: "And the child grew, and waxed strong in spirit, filled with wisdom: and the grace of God was upon him."

Through experience, effort, faithfulness, and the grace of God, we too gain spiritual maturity, wax strong in spirit, and become filled with wisdom. As we serve in a calling, we can develop a heightened sensitivity to the promptings of the Spirit, and thus our wisdom can be enhanced beyond our own understanding.

(Coleen K. Menlove, "Called to Serve," *Ensign*, Sept. 2004, 24.)

MARCH 13
Beware of Envy

And when his brethren saw that their father loved him more than all his brethren, they hated him, and could not speak peaceably unto him.

GENESIS 37:4

See also Prov. 6:34; Rom. 13:13; Alma 16:18.

While they were peaceably and industriously pursuing this object, Satan began to stir up the people around to jealousy, envy and hatred. Mob meetings were held in different parts of the country; resolutions passed, and measures entered into to drive the Saints from their possessions. In the month of November, 1833, a ruthless and murderous mob, composed of many hundreds, armed with weapons of destruction, came suddenly upon the Saints, who were unprepared for defense, and drove men, women and children from their lovely habitations.

(Eliza R. Snow, *Biography and Family Record of Lorenzo Snow* [Salt Lake City: Deseret News, 1884], 146–48.)

MARCH 14

Turn to the Lord in Tribulation

When thou art in tribulation, and all these things are come upon thee, even in the latter days, if thou turn to the Lord thy God, and shalt be obedient unto his voice;

(For the Lord thy God is a merciful God;) he will not forsake thee, neither destroy thee, nor forget the covenant of thy fathers which he sware unto them.

DEUTERONOMY 4:30–31

See also Ex. 3:17.

The Lord told Emma to rejoice. She had much to cause her to rejoice: she was a daughter of God, a member of the Lord's kingdom on the earth, the wife of the Lord's chosen prophet, and an elect lady. In addition, she had the promise that the Lord was with her. He would be her strength in trials and be near to strengthen and comfort her.

The Lord knows each of us better than we know ourselves. He knows our strengths and weaknesses. We each have our free agency; he loves us and wants us to use it wisely.

(Robert L. Millet and Kent P. Jackson, ed., *Studies in Scripture, Vol. 1: The Doctrine and Covenants* [Salt Lake City: Deseret Book, 1989], 126.)

MARCH 15
Overcome Temptation

And she caught him by his garment, saying, Lie with me: and he left his garment in her hand, and fled, and got him out.

GENESIS 39:12.

See also Prov. 1:10; 3:5–6; 1 Ne. 15:24; 3 Ne. 18:18.

We are prone to think that we have temptations and struggles which others have not, but Paul says: "There hath no temptation taken you but such as is common to man: but God is faithful, who will not suffer you to be tempted above that ye are able; but with the temptations also make a way to escape, that ye may be able to bear it."

(Charles A. Callis., *Conference Report*, April 1918, 107.)

MARCH 16

Be Not Deceived by the Spirit of Envy

And his brethren envied him; but his father observed the saying. . . .

And when they saw him afar off, even before he came near unto them, they conspired against him to slay him.

GENESIS 37:11, 18

See also Prov.14:30; 1 Tim. 6:4; Alma 4:9; Ether 9:7.

Brethren and sisters, let us not be deceived. There are many agents of Satan abroad in the land and some of them may be self-deceived, not knowing that they are in the power of the evil one. However, the spirit of the devil among this people may be detected by all honest, sincere members who keep the commandments of the Lord. The spirit of the Lord is comforting, joy-producing, love-inspiring, help-giving. The spirit of the devil is manifested in fault-finding, envy, selfishness, hatred, deceit, dishonesty, and produces misery, sin and crime.

(Joseph F. Merrill, *Conference Report,* April 1941, 51.)

MARCH 17
Consequences of Immorality

Now the sons of Reuben the firstborn of Israel, (for he was the firstborn; but, forasmuch as he defiled his father's bed, his birthright was given unto the sons of Joseph the son of Israel.)

1 Chronicles 5:1

See also Lev. 20:10; Num. 25:1–3; Matt. 5:28; Alma 7:21.

The Church of Jesus Christ of Latter-day Saints teaches the same standard of sexual purity that has been in place among God's people from the beginning of time, including purity of thought, complete sexual abstinence before marriage, and total fidelity within marriage. Following that standard is the only way one can confidently avoid the unfortunate consequences of immorality so prevalent in our society today.

(M. Russell Ballard, *Our Search for Happiness: An Invitation to Understand The Church of Jesus Christ of Latter-day Saints* [Salt Lake City: Deseret Book, 1993], 106.)

MARCH 18
Commitment to Righteousness

Commit thy way unto the Lord; trust also in him; and he shall bring it to pass.

PSALM 37:5

See also Josh. 24:15; 2 Kgs. 23:3.

As I have studied the word *righteousness,* I have found nothing that indicates that being righteous is being perfect. *Goodness, virtue, morality* are all dictionary synonyms, but not *perfect.* All of us will make mistakes in our lives, but although perfection is our ultimate destination, righteousness, or goodness, is the chariot to carry us there. . . .

Every good thing you do in your life is following God's plan. Every time you are kind to another person, each time you have courage to do something difficult, each time you do a thoughtful act without being asked, each time you say your prayers, each time you read the scriptures, each time you go to church, each time you help a friend—you are following God's plan for you.

(Michaelene P. Grassli, "I Will Follow God's Plan for Me," *Ensign,* Nov. 1988, 91–92.)

MARCH 19
Revelation through the Spirit

And Pharaoh said unto his servants, Can we find such a one as this is, a man in whom the Spirit of God is?

GENESIS 41:38

See also Deut. 29:29; Dan. 2:45; John 16:13; 2 Ne. 32:3.

It is necessary that every person should possess the Spirit of revelation, in order to understand and properly appreciate the teachings and instructions given to them by the living oracles of God on earth. Those who are not thus inspired need again to be taught the first principles of the doctrine of Christ.

(Heber C. Kimball, *Journal of Discourses* [London: Latter-day Saints' Book Depot, 1854–1886], 9:298.)

MARCH 20
Looking for the Good

He that diligently seeketh good procureth favour:
but he that seeketh mischief, it shall come unto him.

PROVERBS 11:27

See also Ps. 28:4; Isa. 1:17; Jer. 32:19; Mosiah 5:15.

I am asking that we stop seeking out the storms
and enjoy more fully the sunlight. I am suggesting
that as we go through life we "accentuate the positive." I am asking that we look a little deeper for the
good, that we still voices of insult and sarcasm, that
we more generously compliment virtue and effort. I
am not asking that all criticism be silenced. Growth
comes of correction. Strength comes of repentance.
Wise is the man who can acknowledge mistakes
pointed out by others and change his course.

What I am suggesting is that each of us turn from
the negativism that so permeates our society and look
for the remarkable good among those with whom we
associate, that we speak of one another's virtues more
than we speak of one another's faults, that optimism
replace pessimism, that our faith exceed our fears.

(Gordon B. Hinckley, "The Continuing Pursuit of Truth,"
Ensign, Apr. 1986, 2, 4.)

MARCH 21
Prophecy Fulfilled

And Joseph was the governor over the land, and he it was that sold to all the people of the land: and Joseph's brethren came, and bowed down themselves before him with their faces to the earth.

GENESIS 42:6

See also Gen. 37:5–11; Matt. 13:14; D&C 1:38.

The Lord, speaking through the Prophet Joel, referring to the times when Israel should be gathered in the latter days, said, . . . I will pour out my spirit upon all flesh; and your sons and your daughters shall prophesy, your old men shall dream dreams, your young men shall see visions.

Thousands of Latter-day Saints can testify that this prophecy is being fulfilled and that dreams and visions characterize this as they have former dispensations. This understanding and faith, with its corollary—that to grow and develop, people must dream and have visions—should shape the interest and aspirations of every person.

(Franklin D. Richards, *BYU Speeches of the Year,* 1965, 4.)

MARCH 22
Do Justly

He hath shewed thee, O man, what is good; and what doth the Lord require of thee, but to do justly, and to love mercy, and to walk humbly with thy God?

MICAH 6:8

See also Jer. 17:10; 32:19; Eph. 4:32; Col. 3:12.

I believe that wherever the fullness of the Gospel has been preached, whether by an Adam, an Enoch, a Noah, an Abraham, or a Moses, men have been taught to love each other as the children of God, and to return good for evil.

(Orson F. Whitney, in Brian H. Stuy, ed., *Collected Discourses* [Burbank, CA, and Woodland Hills, UT.: B.H.S. Publishing, 1987–1992], 5:428.)

MARCH 23
Forgiveness Is a Divine Attribute

So shall ye say unto Joseph, Forgive, I pray thee now, the trespass of thy brethren, and their sin; for they did unto thee evil: and now, we pray thee, forgive the trespass of the servants of the God of thy father. And Joseph wept when they spake unto him.

GENESIS 50:17

See also Num. 14:18; D&C 64:10.

Just as repentance is a divine principle, so is forgiveness. The Lord has said, "I, the Lord, will forgive whom I will forgive, but of you it is required to forgive all men." If we were more liberal in our forgiveness, we would be more encouraging to repentance. Someone has said that the supreme charity of the world is in obedience to the divine injunction, "Judge not." When the Savior gave that injunction, he was well aware of the limitations of human understanding and sympathy.

(Stephen L Richards, *Conference Report*, April 1956, 93.)

MARCH 24
The Love of a Parent

And they told him all the words of Joseph, which he had said unto them: and when he saw the wagons which Joseph had sent to carry him, the spirit of Jacob their father revived:

And Israel said, It is enough; Joseph my son is yet alive: I will go and see him before I die.

GENESIS 45:27–28

See also Deut. 6:7; Prov. 3:12; John 5:20; Titus 2:4; 3 Jn. 1:4.

While few human challenges are greater than that of being good parents, few opportunities offer greater potential for joy. Surely no more important work is to be done in this world than preparing our children to be God-fearing, happy, honorable, and productive. . . . In my opinion, the teaching, rearing, and training of children requires more intelligence, intuitive understanding, humility, strength, wisdom, spirituality, perseverance, and hard work than any other challenge we might have in life.

(James E. Faust, "The Greatest Challenge in the World—Good Parenting," *Ensign,* Nov.1990, 32–33.)

MARCH 25
The Lord's Way

Now therefore be not grieved, nor angry with yourselves, that ye sold me hither: for God did send me before you . . . to preserve you a posterity in the earth, and to save your lives by a great deliverance.

So now it was not you that sent me hither, but God.

GENESIS 45:5–8

See also Isa. 55:8–9; 2 Ne. 2:2.

Joseph's brothers determined to sell him rather than to leave him to die. Twenty pieces of silver extricated Joseph from the pit and placed him eventually in . . . the land of Egypt. There Joseph prospered, for "the Lord was with Joseph."

After the years of plenty, there followed the years of famine. In the midst of this latter period, when the brothers of Joseph came to Egypt to buy corn, they were blessed by this favored man in Egypt—even their own brother.

(Thomas S. Monson, "My Brother's Keeper," *Ensign,* May 1990, 46.)

MARCH 26
Affliction—An Essential Part of Life

And the name of the second called he Ephraim:
For God hath caused me to be fruitful in the land of
my affliction.

GENESIS 41:52

See also Lam. 3:1,19; Hosea 5:15; 2 Cor. 2:4; Alma 7:5.

But some will say: "Why, if God is all powerful, does He not restrain the devil, and why does He
allow him to afflict the children of men?" The reason
is found in the fact that these things are necessary.
It is necessary that we should be tempted, that we
should be tried, that we should be purified by going
through these trials and passing through this furnace
of affliction which this life furnishes.

(George Q. Cannon, *Contributor* vol. 11 (November 1889–
October 1890), 478.)

MARCH 27
Trust in the Lord

And I am come down to deliver them out of the hand of the Egyptians, and to bring them up out of that land unto a good land and a large, unto a land flowing with milk and honey; unto the place of the Canaanites, and the Hittites, and the Amorites, and the Perizzites, and the Hivites, and the Jebusites.

EXODUS 3:8

See also Pss. 2:12; 25:2; 2 Ne. 4:34.

It is only those who really put their trust in the Lord, who are thoroughly and firmly grounded in the truth, who are established in the principles of life, that will be able to certainly claim the reward of the faithful, and an exaltation in the presence of the Father. As soon as any man turns away from that witness of the Spirit and from the truth that binds him to God, that moment he is in danger and may fall.

(Joseph F. Smith, *Gospel Doctrine: Selections from the Sermons and Writings of Joseph F. Smith* [Salt Lake City: Deseret Book, 1939], 452.)

MARCH 28
The Atonement of the Lord

The Lord is my strength and song, and he is become my salvation: he is my God, and I will prepare him an habitation; my father's God, and I will exalt him.

EXODUS 15:2

See also Matt. 1:21; 1 Jn. 4:14; 1 Ne. 22:12.

We can never begin to appreciate Christ's infinite atonement until we place our own infinitesimal offering upon the altar by lifting another fellow being. No one can catch the slightest intimation of Jesus' profound love for humanity without becoming involved in service to others—service rendered without hint of recognition or recompense.

(Carlos E. Asay, *Family Pecan Trees: Planting a Legacy of Faith at Home* [Salt Lake City: Deseret Book, 1992], 181.)

MARCH 29

Apply the Atonement to Our Lives

Let the words of my mouth, and the meditation of my heart, be acceptable in thy sight, O Lord, my strength, and my redeemer.

PSALM 19:14

See also Prov. 14:32; Isa. 53:5; Alma 7:11–12; Moro. 10:33.

The third article of faith teaches, "We believe that through the Atonement of Christ, all mankind may be saved, by obedience to the laws and ordinances of the Gospel." The Atonement offers redemption from spiritual death and from suffering caused by sin.

For some reason, we think the Atonement of Christ applies *only* at the end of mortal life to redemption from the Fall, from spiritual death. It is much more than that. It is an ever-present power to call upon in everyday life. When we are racked or harrowed up or tormented by guilt or burdened with grief, He can heal us. While we do not fully understand how the Atonement of Christ was made, we can experience "the peace of God, which passeth all understanding."

(Boyd K. Packer, "The Touch of the Master's Hand," *Ensign*, May 2001, 23.)

MARCH 30
Christ in Your Life

But he that honoureth him hath mercy on the poor.

PROVERBS 14:31

See also Isa. 53:4; Mark 10:21; 2 Ne. 31:16; Moro. 7:48.

Now, understanding charity or being charitable is not easy. And our scriptures have not indicated that it would be. Even "charity suffereth long" requires our thoughtful interpretation. The "suffering" that may come from loving is the result of our great caring. It comes because another matters to us so much.

To avoid that kind of suffering, we would have to avoid what gives us life and hope and joy—our capacity to love deeply. As an antidote against the suffering that will surely come as we have loved ones die, or see them struggle or be misled, or have them misunderstand us or even betray us, we can find relief in charity to others. We accepted bearing one another's burdens and mourning with those who mourn, as we accepted Christ in our baptism. His spirit and power will comfort us as we extend ourselves in help and love to those who need us.

(Aileen H. Clyde, "Charity Suffereth Long," *Ensign*, Nov. 1991, 77.)

MARCH 31

Covenant with the Lord

And when these days are expired, it shall be, that upon the eighth day, and so forward, the priests shall make your burnt offerings upon the altar, and your peace offerings; and I will accept you, saith the Lord God.

EZEKIEL 43:27

See also Gen. 8:20; Ex. 12:27; Lev. 1:3; 1 Ne. 2:7.

President David O. McKay made this choice statement to the Council of the Twelve regarding the blessings of this ordinance: "What a strength there would be in this Church if next Sunday every member who partakes of the Sacrament would sense the significance of the covenant made in that ordinance—every member willing to take upon him the name of the Son, a true Christian proud of it, and always remember him, in the home, in business, in society always remember him and keep his commandments that he has given them. How comprehensive that blessing and how significant the covenant we make each Sabbath day."

(Delbert L. Stapley, *Conference Report,* April 1959, 109.)

APRIL

And ye shall observe this thing for an ordinance
to thee and to thy sons for ever.

—Exodus 12:24

APRIL 1
Forget Not Our Covenants

This is my covenant, which ye shall keep,
between me and you and thy seed after thee.

GENESIS 17:10

See also Jer. 32:40; 50:5; D&C 20: 68–69, 77, 79; 59:9.

It is essential that we renew our covenants by
partaking of the sacrament. When we do this with
a sincere heart, with real intent, forsaking our sins,
and renewing our commitment to God, the Lord
provides a way whereby sins can be forgiven from
week to week. Simply eating the bread and drinking
the water will not bring that forgiveness. We must
prepare and then partake with a broken heart and
contrite spirit. The spiritual preparation we make to
partake of the sacrament is essential to receiving a
remission of our sins.

(Vaughn J. Featherstone, "Sacrament Meeting and the
Sacrament," *Ensign,* Sept. 2001, 24–25.)

APRIL 2
Blessings of Keeping Our Covenants

And he took the book of the covenant, and read in the audience of the people: and they said, All that the Lord hath said will we do, and be obedient.

Exodus 24:7

See also Ps. 119:1; Prov. 3:9–10; Mal. 3:10; Jarom 1:9.

These privileges that are offered to us, holders of the priesthood, just cannot be evaluated. If we keep these covenants, we are blessed. As we go to the temple, we make those covenants that I mentioned before. And I would like to say to you men who hold the priesthood, just remember three words: keep the covenants.

(President N. Eldon Tanner, *Conference Report,* October 1966, 99.)

APRIL 3
Seek the Lord's Help

If my people, which are called by my name, shall humble themselves, and pray, and seek my face, and turn from their wicked ways; then will I hear from heaven, and will forgive their sin, and will heal their land.

2 CHRONICLES 7:14

See also Isa. 26:9; Mark 11:24; John 16:23.

How can we build that kind of faith in the strength of the Savior? David had counsel for the people of his time that I repeat to you: "Seek the Lord and his strength, seek his face continually. Remember his marvellous works that he hath done, his wonders, and the judgments of his mouth." "Blessed is the man [or woman] whose strength is in thee; in whose heart are [thy] ways. . . . Go from strength to strength." Strengthen yourselves by seeking the source of true strength: the Savior. Come unto him. He loves you. He desires your happiness and exults in your desires for righteousness.

(Chieko N. Okazaki, *Aloha!* [Salt Lake City: Deseret Book, 1995], 13–14.)

APRIL 4

The Lord Will Provide

And Moses said unto the people, Fear ye not, stand still, and see the salvation of the Lord, which he will shew to you to day: for the Egyptians whom ye have seen to day, ye shall see them again no more for ever.

The Lord shall fight for you, and ye shall hold your peace.

EXODUS 14:13–14

See also 2 Sam. 22:3; 1 Ne. 3:7; 17:3; Ether 12:27.

We are told by him that it is his business to provide for his Saints. Now the better Saints we are, the better the Lord will provide for us.

(Charles C. Rich, *Journal of Discourses* [London: Latter-day Saints' Book Depot, 1854–1886], 19:257.)

APRIL 5
Remember the Lord's Goodness and Mercy

Nevertheless for thy great mercies' sake thou didst not utterly consume them, nor forsake them; for thou art a gracious and merciful God.

NEHEMIAH 9:31

See also Pss. 25:7; 102:13; Luke 1:72.

There is no surer way to remember the Lord, His goodness and mercy, than to serve His children who want and have not.

(George Reynolds and Janne M. Sjodahl, *Commentary on the Book of Mormon* [Salt Lake City: Deseret Book, 1955–1961], 2:73.)

APRIL 6
We Are Dependent on the Lord

And Moses stretched out his hand over the sea; and the Lord caused the sea to go back by a strong east wind all that night, and made the sea dry land, and the waters were divided.

EXODUS 14:21

See also Ex. 15:2; Prov. 3:26; 2 Ne. 4:19.

I have a feeling that many of us go through our days trying to resolve our own problems—spiritual, temporal, and otherwise—and do not turn to the Lord as we should. We can receive all sorts of blessings from the Lord, but we must ask, we must ask in faith, and we must know that we are utterly dependent on the Lord for all our support.

(Gene R. Cook, *Receiving Answers to Our Prayers* [Salt Lake City: Deseret Book, 1996], 53.)

APRIL 7
Rely on the Lord

Blessed is the man whose strength is in thee.

PSALM 84:5

See also Ex. 14:13–14; Ps. 27:1; Alma 26:12.

Above all else, may we ever remember that we do not go forth alone to battle the Goliaths of our lives. As David declared to Israel, so might we echo the knowledge, "The battle is the Lord's, and he will give [Goliath] into our hands." But the battle must be fought. Victory cannot come by default. So it is in the battles of life. Life will never spread itself in an unobstructed view before us. We must anticipate the approaching forks and turnings in the road. We cannot hope to reach our desired journey's end if we think aimlessly about whether to go east or west. We must make our decisions purposefully. Our most significant opportunities will be found in times of greatest difficulty.

(Thomas S. Monson, "Meeting Your Goliath," *Ensign,* Jan. 1987, 5.)

APRIL 8
Sustain Our Leaders

But Moses' hands were heavy; and they took a stone, and put it under him, and he sat thereon; and Aaron and Hur stayed up his hands, the one on the one side, and the other on the other side; and his hands were steady until the going down of the sun.

Exodus 17:12

See also 2 Chr. 20:20; Heb. 13:17; D&C 107:22.

[My mother] never spoke ill of any person, and so if I follow her example, I cannot speak ill of any person either. She always taught us to sustain our bishop and our stake president and the General Authorities. She said that if we did not sustain our leaders, we were not sustaining our God, because they are the representatives of the Lord. She also taught us that when we criticize the leaders of the Church, we are on the road to apostasy. I have tried to follow my mother's teachings in this regard.

(James E. Faust, *To Reach Even unto You* [Salt Lake City: Deseret Book, 1980], 65.)

APRIL 9
Blessings of Obedience

Now therefore, if ye will obey my voice indeed, and keep my covenant, then ye shall be a peculiar treasure unto me above all people: for all the earth is mine.

EXODUS 19:5

See also Gen. 22:18; Deut. 30:20; Luke 11:28; 3 Ne. 10:18.

We are blessed for keeping the commandments of the Lord with all that he has given us, which, if we will follow and be true and faithful, will bring us back again into the presence of God our Eternal Father, as sons and daughters of God, entitled to the fullness of celestial glory.

(Joseph Fielding Smith, *Conference Report*, October 1967, 122.)

APRIL 10
Overcome the Appetite for Worldly Pleasures

And the mixt multitude that was among them fell a lusting: and the children of Israel also wept again, and said, Who shall give us flesh to eat?

We remember the fish, which we did eat in Egypt freely; the cucumbers, and the melons, and the leeks, and the onions, and the garlick:

But now our soul is dried away: there is nothing at all, beside this manna, before our eyes.

NUMBERS 11:4–6

See also Matt. 13:22; D&C 25:10.

The first recorded question of the Savior after his baptism in the river Jordan, was, "What seekest thou?" In the text I have just read [Matt. 16:26] he again refers to the dominant incentive prompting man's actions in daily life. If a man seek wealth, worldly honors, pleasures and all that riches and honor can bestow but neglects and leaves undeveloped the eternal riches of his soul, what is he profited? Thus does the Lord emphasize in a simple though majestic comparison of material and spiritual possessions.

(David O. McKay, *Conference Report,* April 1953, 14.)

APRIL 11
Murmur Not

And all the children of Israel murmured against Moses and against Aaron: and the whole congregation said unto them, Would God that we had died in the land of Egypt! or would God we had died in this wilderness!

NUMBERS 14:2

See also John 6:43; 1 Ne. 17:49.

It is one thing to bear up under the wrongs of the wicked; it sometimes is quite another to rise above the offenses given by one's fellow saints. Hence the counsel: Do not murmur or grumble or manifest harsh judgment against the brethren.

(Bruce R. McConkie, *Doctrinal New Testament Commentary* [Salt Lake City: Bookcraft, 1965–1973], 3:272.)

APRIL 12
Don't Speak Against the Lord's Anointed

And the anger of the Lord was kindled against them, and he departed.

NUMBERS 12:9

See also Acts 23:5; Eph. 4:31; James 4:11; D&C 20:54.

Faultfinding, evil speaking, and backbiting are obviously unchristian. The Bible commands us to avoid "evil speakings." It tells us to "Let all bitterness, and wrath, and anger, and clamour, and evil speaking, be put away from you." Modern revelations direct us to avoid "backbiting," "evil speaking," and "find[ing] fault one with another."

We are given these commandments for a reason. The Apostle Paul advised the Saints to "grieve not the holy Spirit of God" by evil speaking. . . . Does the commandment to avoid faultfinding and evil speaking apply to Church members' destructive personal criticism of Church leaders? Of course it does. It applies to criticism of all Church leaders—local or general, male or female. In our relations with all of our Church leaders, we should follow the Apostle Paul's direction: "Rebuke not an elder, but intreat him as a father."

(Dallin H. Oaks, "Criticism," *Ensign,* Feb. 1987, 68, 70.)

APRIL 13
Overcome Fear and Doubt

Only rebel not ye against the Lord, neither fear ye the people of the land; for they are bread for us: their defence is departed from them, and the Lord is with us: fear them not.

NUMBERS 14:9
See also Gen. 15:1; Ex. 20:20; 2 Tim. 1:7; D&C 3:7.

With the Holy Ghost dwelling in us, we feel a love for God and all His children. This love casts out fear and fills us with the desire to open our mouths. There is no greater gift we can give others than to bear our testimony to them. There is no greater joy we can have than to bring even one soul unto Christ. And there is no greater way to strengthen our own testimony than to share our witness of Him with the world. As we do, our families will be strengthened. Our wards, stakes, and communities will be filled with peace and love, and, ultimately, the earth will be prepared for the Second Coming of our Lord and Savior Jesus Christ.

(Robert D. Hales, "Receiving a Testimony of the Restored Gospel of Jesus Christ," *Ensign,* Nov. 2003, 31.)

APRIL 14
Power in Meekness

Now the man Moses was very meek, above all the men which were upon the face of the earth.

NUMBERS 12:3

See also Ps. 37:11; 2 Ne. 27:30; Moro. 8:26.

Let Jesus be our exemplar in this and all other aspects of our leadership responsibilities. Always meek and humble, He never succumbed to the temptation to abuse power and authority. Humility and meekness are the keys to avoiding the corruption of power.

(Alexander B. Morrison, *Feed My Sheep: Leadership Ideas for Latter-day Shepherds* [Salt Lake City: Deseret Book, 1992], 173.)

APRIL 15
Feast upon the Word and Come unto Christ

And he humbled thee, and suffered thee to hunger, and fed thee with manna, which thou knewest not, neither did thy fathers know; that he might make thee know that man doth not live by bread only, but by every word that proceedeth out of the mouth of the Lord doth man live.

DEUTERONOMY 8:3

See also Josh. 8:34; John 5:39; 2 Ne. 32:3. Alma 37:44–47.

[God] has commanded us to read them, to feast upon the word. We must feast upon his word in order to understand our responsibilities. We can't just nibble.

Elder J. Richard Clarke has written, "The holy scriptures are the word of God. If we are to know God, we must read His words, for therein He stands revealed to the honest heart."

(Joseph B. Wirthlin, *Finding Peace in Our Lives* [Salt Lake City: Deseret Book, 1995], 164.)

APRIL 16
Look to God and Live

And the Lord said unto Moses, Make thee a fiery serpent, and set it upon a pole: and it shall come to pass, that every one that is bitten, when he looketh upon it, shall live.

And Moses made a serpent of brass, and put it upon a pole, and it came to pass, that if a serpent had bitten any man, when he beheld the serpent of brass, he lived.

NUMBERS 21:8–9

See also 2 Sam. 22:31; Alma 33:18–19; Hel. 8:13–14.

If, in addition to living righteously, we will study and learn what the Lord has said and apply the tests I have suggested, we shall never go astray. God help us, I pray, that we shall remain true and faithful ourselves and help all of the members of the Church to see clearly, thereby placing themselves among those who, taking the Holy Spirit for their guide, are not deceived but look to God and live.

(Marion G. Romney, *Look to God and Live* [Salt Lake City: Deseret Book, 1971], 63.)

APRIL 17

Obey the Word of God

And Balaam answered and said unto the servants of Balak, If Balak would give me his house full of silver and gold, I cannot go beyond the word of the Lord my God, to do less or more.

NUMBERS 22:18

See also Isa. 30:8; 2 Tim. 3:16; 1 Ne. 19:23.

If you want to obtain a knowledge that this work is of God, obey the word of God, and you shall receive the gift of the Holy Ghost; and when you receive that gift, you will know: you will be beyond belief, so far as that one thing is concerned. You will know that this is the truth which we have told you: you will know that an angel of God has been sent from heaven; that the Book of Mormon is a Divine revelation—the history of ancient America, containing the Gospel preached in ancient times in this land; that God has raised up his kingdom on earth for the last time.

(Orson Pratt, *Journal of Discourses* [London: Latter-day Saints' Book Depot, 1854–1886], 7:266.)

APRIL 18

When the Lord Speaks, Obey

But Balaam answered and said unto Balak, Told not I thee, saying, All that the Lord speaketh, that I must do?

NUMBERS 23:26

See also Num. 23:12; Ps. 95:7–8; D&C 103:7.

He gave his life a ransom to atone for the sins of the world, and he has pointed out the way. His law is sacred, omnipotent, eternal; and that is the law to obey. Let the Lord speak, and let the people obey. That is the way to gain that happiness which all mankind are seeking, and no other course can satisfy the noble, Godlike spirit placed in man, who is formed for the express purpose of preserving his identity to all eternity. Without strict observance to the laws by which worlds were and are created—to the words of the Eternal, no being can inherit eternal lives.

(Brigham Young, *Journal of Discourses* [London: Latter-day Saints' Book Depot, 1854–1886], 7:3–4.)

APRIL 19
Submit Your Will to the Lord

Lord, thou hast heard the desire of the humble: thou wilt prepare their heart, thou wilt cause thine ear to hear:

PSALM 10:17

See also Gen. 16:9; Ex. 10:3; Luke 22:41–42; Mosiah 3:19.

Sometimes we must deliberately put aside the cares of the world, put aside the rush of our daily lives, and find a quiet place and a quiet time where we can sit and ponder and reflect and meditate—and listen for that still small voice that whispers. Part of that time of pondering will be to deliberately push your wants down. You will remind yourself that it is not your place to counsel the Lord or to try and tell him what is best for you. You will consciously remember the Gethsemane principle . . . and submit your will to his.

(Gerald N. Lund, *Selected Writings of Gerald N. Lund: Gospel Scholars Series* [Salt Lake City: Deseret Book, 1999], 284.)

APRIL 20
Whom the Lord Loves He Chastens

My son, despise not the chastening of the Lord;
neither be weary of his correction.

PROVERBS 3:11

See also Num. 22:32, 34; Heb. 12:6; D&C 95:1–2.

Paul, the ancient apostle, reminds us of this
exhortation: "My son, despise not thou the chastening of the Lord, nor faint when thou art rebuked of
him: for whom the Lord loveth he chasteneth." He
adds: "No chastening for the present seemeth to be
joyous, but grievous: nevertheless afterward it yield-
eth the peaceable fruit of righteousness unto them
which are exercised thereby." Parents, like the Lord,
love their children. Therefore they chasten their sons
and daughters when they are in need of correction.
This is not done because it brings Mother and Dad
pleasure, but because they want to spare their young
ones unnecessary suffering and sorrow.

(Carlos E. Asay, *The Road to Somewhere: A Guide for Young
Men and Women* [Salt Lake City: Bookcraft, 1994], 89.)

APRIL 21
Tempting Others Is Sin

Behold, these caused the children of Israel, through the counsel of Balaam, to commit trespass against the Lord in the matter of Peor, and there was a plague among the congregation of the Lord.

NUMBERS 31:16

See also Deut. 13:6; Prov. 1:10; Jacob 2:35; Mosiah 21:30; Alma 39:11.

The record of Zeniff's people told how wicked King Noah led his subjects into all manner of sin. Noah's wanton practices became examples for his people to follow. Although at first the debaucheries of his court brought seeming pleasure to many of his followers, they ended in sorrow, in fierce bondage to the Lamanites in which murder, pillage, rapine, theft, and every cruelty which the ingenuity of their masters could suggest or evil power achieve was made part.

(George Reynolds and Janne M. Sjodahl, *Commentary on the Book of Mormon* [Salt Lake City: Deseret Book, 1955–1961], 4:214.)

APRIL 22
Power of Example

But the path of the just is as the shining light,
that shineth more and more unto the perfect day.

PROVERBS 4:18

See also Gen. 39:8; Josh. 24:15; 2 Ne. 31:16; 3 Ne. 18:16.

Because our greatest need is for God, our
relationship to him becomes the first and the most
important commandment. And the commandment
second in importance has been built around our
second greatest need, which is for the good will and
inspiration of other people. The greatest power in
the world is the power of love, and we ought to build
more love into our lives. The second greatest power
is the power of example. One of our greatest assets is
to have some good working models of righteousness.

(Sterling W. Sill, *BYU Speeches of the Year*, 1962, 2.)

APRIL 23
Seek to Honor the Lord

Thou shalt have no other gods before me. . . .

For I the Lord thy God am a jealous God, visiting the iniquity of the fathers upon the children unto the third and fourth generation of them that hate me;

And shewing mercy unto thousands of them that love me, and keep my commandments.

EXODUS 20:3, 5–6

See also Prov. 3:9; 1 Jn. 2:15; Alma 4:8; D&C 121:35.

If individuals are more concerned with pleasing men than pleasing God, then they suffer from the same virus Satan had, for there are many situations where seeking the praise of men will clearly result in their hurting, not helping, mankind for they will do expedient and temporary things instead of those which are lasting and beneficial.

How much more satisfying it is when we receive the praise of God, knowing that it is fully justified and that his love and respect for us will persist, when usually the praise of men is fleeting and most disappointing.

(N. Eldon Tanner, "For They Loved the Praise of Men More Than the Praise of God," *Ensign,* Nov. 1975, 74.)

APRIL 24
Remember the Commandments

And thou shalt bind them for a sign upon thine hand, and they shall be as frontlets between thine eyes.

And thou shalt write them upon the posts of thy house, and on thy gates.

DEUTERONOMY 6:8–9

See also Num. 15:39; Deut. 5:31; 1 Jn. 3:23.

We are the Lord's people, his saints, those to whom he has given much and from whom he expects much in return. We know the terms and conditions of the plan of salvation—how Christ died for our sins and what we must do to reap the full blessings of his atoning sacrifice.

We have covenanted in the waters of baptism to love and serve him, to keep his commandments, and to put first in our lives the things of his kingdom. In return he has promised us eternal life in his Father's kingdom. We are thus in a position to receive and obey some of the higher laws which prepare us for that eternal life which we so sincerely seek.

(Bruce R. McConkie, "Obedience, Consecration, and Sacrifice," *Ensign,* May 1975, 50.)

APRIL 25
The Lord Will Not Forsake Us

(For the Lord thy God is a merciful God;) he will not forsake thee, neither destroy thee, nor forget the covenant of thy fathers which he sware unto them.

DEUTERONOMY 4:31

See also 1 Sam. 12:22; Pss. 9:10; 27:10.

Sometimes we meet with reverses and we are brought face to face with our inability to do things without divine help, but if we will humble ourselves and put our trust in the Lord, he will not forsake us. The path of humility is always the path of safety for the members of the Church.

(George Albert Smith, *Conference Report,* April 1923, 78.)

APRIL 26
Never Forsake the Lord

And the people answered and said, God forbid
that we should forsake the Lord, to serve other gods.

JOSHUA 24:16

See also Josh. 24:20; Jer. 17:13; Alma 46:21; Hel. 12:2–3.

I received many birthday cards for my eighty-
third birthday in March of 1978. One was bound in
a book and had 4,700 autographs of youths who had
signed the book. They were pledging their lives with
such statements as the following:

"I pledge to you and the Lord to lengthen my
stride, to quicken my pace, to stretch my soul in the
work of the Lord."

"I promise to remember my nightly and morning
prayers. I shall never forget the Lord nor his rich promises, his protecting care, and his rich blessings." . . .

Now, brothers and sisters, you are sweet and
wonderful, and we are proud of you, proud of the
records you make, proud of the devotion you show,
proud of the sacrifice you make.

(Spencer W. Kimball, *President Kimball Speaks Out* [Salt
Lake City: Deseret Book, 1981], 16.)

Withstand Temptation

If thy brother, the son of thy mother, or thy son, or thy daughter, or the wife of thy bosom, or thy friend, which is as thine own soul, entice thee secretly, saying, Let us go and serve other gods, which thou hast not known, thou, nor thy fathers . . .

Thou shalt not consent unto him, nor hearken unto him.

DEUTERONOMY 13:6, 8

See also Prov. 1:10; Alma 37:33; D&C 20:33.

Then they will be prepared to have the Holy Ghost conferred upon them with all its powers, gifts, and blessings, . . . which made them such mighty men in the midst of an unbelieving world. . . . It gave them strength to withstand every temptation and to pass through every trial, still clinging to the faith which God had given them—that faith which brings out of trouble, salvation and blessing.

(Abraham H. Cannon in Brian H. Stuy, ed., *Collected Discourses* [Burbank, CA, and Woodland Hills, UT: B.H.S. Publishing, 1987–1992], 4:1.)

APRIL 28
Rock of Our Salvation

Because I will publish the name of the Lord:
ascribe ye greatness unto our God.

He is the Rock, his work is perfect: for all his
ways are judgment: a God of truth and without iniquity, just and right is he.

DEUTERONOMY 32:3–4

See also Ps. 62:2, 6; Hel. 5:12.

Jesus Christ is the rock of our salvation, the sure
and solid foundation "whereon if men build they
cannot fall." One comes unto Christ through accepting and obeying the word of his anointed servants,
repenting of sin, receiving the ordinances of salvation, and enduring in faith to the end.

(Joseph Fielding McConkie and Robert L. Millet, *Doctrinal
Commentary on the Book of Mormon* [Salt Lake City: Bookcraft,
1987–1992], 1:262.)

APRIL 29
Build upon the Rock

He shall cry unto me, Thou art my father, my God, and the rock of my salvation.

PSALM 89:26

See also Ex. 15:2; Ps. 27:1; 3 Ne. 18:13; D&C 11:24; 33:13.

All that we do as members of The Church of Jesus Christ of Latter-day Saints must be built upon a foundation of faith and testimony and conversion. When external supports fail us, then our hearts must be riveted upon the things of the Spirit, those internal realities which provide the meaning, the perspective, and the sustenance for all else that matters in life.

(Robert L. Millet, "The Only Sure Foundation: Building on the Rock of Our Redeemer" in Monte S. Nyman and Charles D. Tate, Jr., ed., *Helaman through 3 Nephi 8: According to Thy Word* [Provo: BYU Religious Studies Center, 1992], 27.)

APRIL 30
Remember Your Covenants

To such as keep his covenant, and to those that remember his commandments to do them.

The Lord hath prepared his throne in the heavens; and his kingdom ruleth over all.

PSALM 103:18–19

See also Jer. 14:21; D&C 33:14; 84:57.

Be faithful to your religion. Remember your covenants. Eschew all impure thoughts and feelings and live humbly and prayerfully before the Lord, and that you may be greatly blessed and prospered in the ministry and return unspotted from the world.

(Brigham Young, *Letters of Brigham Young to His Sons* [Salt Lake City: Deseret Book, 1974], 135.)

MAY

*And they sacrificed sacrifices unto
the Lord . . .*

—1 Chronicles 29:21

MAY 1
The Lord Is with Us

There shall not any man be able to stand before thee all the days of thy life: as I was with Moses, so I will be with thee: I will not fail thee, nor forsake thee.

JOSHUA 1:5

See also Gen. 26:28; Josh. 6:27; 2 Tim. 4:17; 1 Ne. 16:39.

There are many things that are consoling; and one is, to know that the Lord is with us—that he does reveal his mind and will in the ordinances of the house of God, and through the administration of blessings whether by Patriarchs, or by the Twelve Apostles, or in the endowments. We find those blessings are fulfilled to the very letter.

(Wilford Woodruff, *Journal of Discourses* [London: Latter-day Saints' Book Depot, 1854–1886], 5:267.)

MAY 2
Be Strong and Courageous

Only be thou strong and very courageous, that thou mayest observe to do according to all the law, which Moses my servant commanded thee: turn not from it to the right hand or to the left, that thou mayest prosper whithersoever thou goest.

Joshua 1:7

See also Deut. 20:1; 2 Sam. 13:28; Alma 53:20.

Foster your faith. Fuse your focus with an eye single to the glory of God. "Be strong and courageous," and you will be given power and protection from on high. "For I will go before your face," the Lord declared. "I will be on your right hand and on your left, and my Spirit shall be in your hearts, and mine angels round about you, to bear you up."

The great latter-day work of which we are a part shall be accomplished. Prophecies of the ages shall be fulfilled. "For with God all things are possible."

(Russell M. Nelson, *Hope* [Salt Lake City: Deseret Book, 1994], 44–45.)

MAY 3

Ponder and Do the Things of the Lord

This book of the law shall not depart out of thy mouth; but thou shalt meditate therein day and night, that thou mayest observe to do according to all that is written therein: for then thou shalt make thy way prosperous, and then thou shalt have good success.

JOSHUA 1:8

See also Ps. 119:15; Prov. 4:26; 1 Ne. 11:1; D&C 138:1–11.

I do want to add one more important point, however. *Pondering is a form of prayer.* Pondering and prayer are so tightly linked that when I start to ponder I automatically offer a silent prayer: "Help me understand this, Heavenly Father. Help me to know what this means. I'm anxious to change." I have offered such a prayer many times. "I want to repent. I want to change. I want to be better. Help me understand what I should do next."

(Gene R. Cook, *Searching the Scriptures: Bringing Power to Your Personal and Family Study* [Salt Lake City: Deseret Book, 1997], 54.)

MAY 4

Sanctification through the Lord

And Joshua said unto the people, Sanctify yourselves: for to morrow the Lord will do wonders among you.

JOSHUA 3:5

See also Ezek. 20:12; 1 Cor.1:2; Alma 5:54; Hel. 3:35.

The Holy Ghost will, with edifying, instructive and corrective revelations to the heart and mind of man and woman, lead them because of their personal faith through a cleansing process until their sins are remitted. This process of sanctification in Jesus Christ, when completed, becomes a key to obtaining great knowledge, for "in that day that they shall exercise faith in me, saith the Lord . . . that they may become sanctified in me, then I will manifest unto them the things which the brother of Jared saw, even to the unfolding unto them all my revelations."

(Robert L. Millet, in Monte S. Nyman and Charles D. Tate, Jr., ed., *Fourth Nephi through Moroni: From Zion to Destruction* [Provo: BYU Religious Studies Center, 1995], 35.)

MAY 5
Cleave unto the Lord

But cleave unto the Lord your God, as ye have done unto this day.

JOSHUA 23:8

See also Deut. 4:4; Acts 11:23; Hel. 4:25.

Let us cleave unto the Lord and walk in His ways; strive to serve Him in all things, that we may be able to increase in righteousness; that we and our generations after us may grow up in fear of the Lord, honor Him in the earth, and be counted worthy of that life and immortality which are being brought to light in the Gospel, and which the Savior has died to bring to pass unto us.

(Franklin D. Richards, *Conference Report,* April 1899, 48.)

MAY 6
Follow the Lord

Nevertheless my brethren that went up with me made the heart of the people melt: but I wholly followed the Lord my God.

JOSHUA 14:8

See also 1 Sam. 25:27; Matt. 19:21; Luke 9:57–61.

If and when there is a conflict of interest between members' earthly pursuits and their heavenly pursuits, it is time to take stock and choose to walk in the course charted from on high. The Saints' chief obligation is to follow the Lord and work for his interests. Their pledge, sworn on the altars of God, is and must be that they will never do anything to destroy faith; they must never perform an act or espouse a cause that runs counter to the needs and purposes of the Church. If this means they forsake the course their colleagues in the world pursue, so be it. Each member must come to believe and declare with soberness: "The kingdom of God or nothing!"

(Joseph Fielding McConkie and Robert L. Millet, *Doctrinal Commentary on the Book of Mormon* [Salt Lake City: Bookcraft, 1987–1992], 1:346.)

MAY 7
Choose to Serve the Lord

And if it seem evil unto you to serve the Lord, choose you this day whom ye will serve; whether the gods which your fathers served that were on the other side of the flood, or the gods of the Amorites, in whose land ye dwell: but as for me and my house, we will serve the Lord.

JOSHUA 24:15

See also Deut. 10:12; Josh. 24:22–24; 1 Sam. 12:14; Ps. 100:2.

May our youth prepare for their roles in life. May they choose and prepare for a mission in their future. May they choose and prepare for marriage in the house of God. May they choose to honor father and mother. May they choose to serve the Lord in accordance with His great gift of free agency. . . . This is the key that will unlock the treasure chest of knowledge and inspiration to every young man and to every young woman. May youth of the noble birthright ever choose the Lord's way!

(Thomas S. Monson, *Be Your Best Self* [Salt Lake City: Deseret Book, 1979], 84.)

MAY 8
Seek First the Lord

And they forsook the Lord God of their fathers, which brought them out of the land of Egypt, and followed other gods, . . .

And the anger of the Lord was hot against Israel, and he delivered them into the hands of spoilers that spoiled them, and he sold them into the hands of their enemies round about, so that they could not any longer stand before their enemies.

JUDGES 2:12, 14

See also Isa.1:28.

What we seek first and foremost, above all other things, is "the kingdom of God, and his righteousness." We seek to know "the only true God and Jesus Christ whom [He has] sent."

In a very personal version of the invitation to seek and find, the Savior said, "Draw near unto me and I will draw near unto you; seek me diligently and ye shall find me."

(Craig C. Christensen, "Seek, and Ye Shall Find," *Ensign,* May 2003, 33.)

MAY 9

Obey with the Assurance of the Lord

And the Lord looked upon him, and said, Go in this thy might, and thou shalt save Israel from the hand of the Midianites: have not I sent thee?

JUDGES 6:14

See also Pss. 34:22; 37:3; 62:8; John 17:2; Moses 6:61.

The Lord answered their prayers, and abode with them by His Spirit. He comforted them with the assurance of ultimate success in their heartfelt desire to extend His Kingdom among the Lamanites, who then were "a wild and a hardened and a ferocious people." . . . Urged on by the assurance of the Lord, and earnestly relying upon His goodness, the missionaries continued their wanderings, and before long reached the end of their protracted journey, the Land of Nephi, where the main body of the Lamanites dwelt.

(George Reynolds and Janne M. Sjodahl, *Commentary on the Book of Mormon* [Salt Lake City: Deseret Book, 1955–1961], 3:245–46.)

MAY 10
Be a True and Loyal Friend

A friend loveth at all times, and a brother is born for adversity.

PROVERBS 17:17

See also Prov. 18:24; John 15:13; D&C 121:9.

Mothers, take time to be a real friend to your children. Listen to your children, really listen. Talk with them, laugh and joke with them, sing with them, play with them, cry with them, hug them, honestly praise them. Yes, regularly spend unrushed one-on-one time with each child. Be a real friend to your children.

(Ezra Taft Benson, *Come, Listen to a Prophet's Voice* [Salt Lake City: Deseret Book, 1990], 32.)

MAY 11
God Is a God of Miracles

I will praise thee, O Lord, with my whole heart;
I will shew forth all thy marvellous works.

PSALM 9:1

See also Ex. 3:20; 34:10; Ps. 77:14; 2 Ne. 27:23; D&C 35:8.

Among the signs of the true church, and included in the evidences of God's work in the world, are the manifestations of his power which we are helpless to explain or to fully understand. In the scriptures these divine acts and special blessings are variously referred to as miracles or signs or wonders or marvels.

Not surprisingly, these signs and marvels were most evident in the life and ministry of Jesus Christ, the very Son of God himself. But startling and wonder-filled as they were, Christ's many miracles were only reflections of those greater marvels which his Father had performed before him and continues to perform all around us. Indeed, the Savior's humble performance of such obviously divine acts may be just one very special application of the declarations he made:

(Howard W. Hunter, "The God That Doest Wonders," *Ensign,* May 1989, 15–16.)

MAY 12
The Strength of the Lord

And he shall stand and feed in the strength of the Lord, in the majesty of the name of the Lord his God; and they shall abide: for now shall he be great unto the ends of the earth.

MICAH 5:4

See also Pss. 27:1; 84:5; Hab. 3:19; Alma 20:4.

What a glorious promise! In overcoming limitations through the grace of Jesus Christ, our opportunity is to be among the weak things that become strong in the strength of the Lord. Let us claim that promise!

(Chieko N. Okazaki, *Lighten Up!* [Salt Lake City: Deseret Book, 1993], 51.)

MAY 13

Separate Yourself from the Sins of the World

Depart from me, all ye workers of iniquity; for the LORD hath heard the voice of my weeping.

PSALM 6:8

See also Deut. 9:4; Alma 5:57; D&C 1:16; 133:5.

The Lord would have His people separate themselves from the sins of the world and depart from spiritual Babylon, that they may learn the ways of God and serve Him the more fully.

(James E. Talmage, *Articles of Faith* [Salt Lake City: Deseret Book, 1981], 306.)

MAY 14
Magnificent Mothers

Therefore I will judge you, O house of Israel, every one according to his ways, saith the Lord God. Repent, and turn yourselves from all your transgressions; so iniquity shall not be your ruin.

Cast away from you all your transgressions, whereby ye have transgressed; and make you a new heart and a new spirit: for why will ye die, O house of Israel?

EZEKIEL 18:30–31

See also Prov. 31:1; Alma 56:47.

Now God bless our wonderful mothers. We pray for you. We sustain you. We honor you as you bear, nourish, train, teach, and love for eternity. I promise you the blessings of heaven and "all that [the] Father hath" as you magnify the noblest calling of all—a mother in Zion.

(Ezra Taft Benson, *Come, Listen to a Prophet's Voice* [Salt Lake City: Deseret Book, 1990], 37.)

MAY 15
Love Thy Neighbor

Thou shalt not avenge, nor bear any grudge against the children of thy people, but thou shalt love thy neighbour as thyself: I am the Lord.

LEVITICUS 19:18

See also Ex. 22:21; Isa. 1:17; Zech. 7:9; Matt. 25:40.

The caring for the poor and the handicapped and those who need our help is a main purpose and an absolute requirement in fulfilling the royal law of loving our neighbors as ourselves. You will remember the great sermon of Amulek on prayer, in which he tells the people to pray and tells them how often to pray— morning, night, and noon—and tells them where to pray and how to pray and what to pray for. He goes into great detail and then he says that "after ye have done all these things, if ye turn away the needy, and the naked, and visit not the sick and afflicted, and impart of your substance, if ye have, to those who stand in need—I say unto you, if ye do not any of these things, behold, your prayer is vain, and availeth you nothing, and ye are as hypocrites who do deny the faith."

(Marion G. Romney, "The Royal Law of Love," *Ensign,* May 1978, 95.)

MAY 16
Sacrifice for Righteousness

And Abel, he also brought of the firstlings of his flock and of the fat thereof. And the Lord had respect unto Abel and to his offering.

GENESIS 4:4

See also Ex. 20:24; Lev. 19:5; Ps. 50:4–6; Luke 17:33.

What made their lives a sacrifice for righteousness was not in dying for the faith but in living for it. As Paul admonished, "I beseech you therefore, brethren, by the mercies of God, that ye present your bodies a living sacrifice, holy, acceptable unto God which is your reasonable service."

(Richard D. Draper, *Opening the Seven Seals: The Visions of John the Revelator* [Salt Lake City: Deseret Book, 1991], 69.)

MAY 17
Diligence

But take diligent heed to do the commandment and the law, which Moses the servant of the Lord charged you, to love the Lord your God, and to walk in all his ways, and to keep his commandments, and to cleave unto him, and to serve him with all your heart and with all your soul.

JOSHUA 22:5

See also Ex. 15:26; Deut. 6:17; Isa. 55:2; Moro. 9:6.

Success requires diligent effort. Success is not like manna that falls every working day alike on the worker and the shiftless, on the resourceful one and the careless one. Success is reserved for those who work at it, those not afraid of the midnight oil.

(Spencer W. Kimball, *The Teachings of Spencer W. Kimball* [Salt Lake City: Bookcraft, 1982], 359–60.)

MAY 18
Kindness

And David said, Is there yet any that is left of the house of Saul, that I may shew him kindness for Jonathan's sake?

2 SAMUEL 9:1

See also Prov. 31:26; Luke 10:33–35; Eph. 4:32; Moro. 7:45.

Love begets love, and kindness, kindness. One can scarcely expect to reap what he does not sow. Win the confidence of all men by uprightness, in walk and conversation.

(Joseph F. Smith, *From Prophet to Son: Advice of Joseph F. Smith to His Missionary Sons* [Salt Lake City: Deseret Book, 1981], 106.)

MAY 19
Honesty

Thou shalt not bear false witness against thy neighbour.

EXODUS 20:16

See also Lev. 19:12; Job 27:4; Ps. 31:18; Eph. 4:25.

I want my sons to realize and would be glad if all the world could understand that no matter whether a man is a lawyer, a doctor, a mechanic, or indeed, be he engaged in any occupation whatever, that thorough honesty and integrity will always lead to success, influence, and respect. If a young man wishes to prosper in his profession, this is the only sure road to progress.

(Brigham Young, *Letters of Brigham Young to His Sons* [Salt Lake City: Deseret Book, 1974], 222.)

MAY 20
Build Temples unto the Lord

And let them make me a sanctuary; that I may dwell among them.

EXODUS 25:8

See also 2 Sam. 7:5; 1 Chr. 22:6; D&C 97:15-16; 109:8.

Now, I'd like to submit to you that when all is said and done, the work and the mission of this Church is to save. It's just that simple and just that profound . . . to save people. That's the whole purpose of what we are doing. . . . That's why we build temples, to save the living and the dead. That's our work. "This is my work and my glory—to bring to pass the immortality and eternal life of man."

(Gordon B. Hinckley, *Teachings of Gordon B. Hinckley* [Salt Lake City: Deseret Book, 1997], 119.)

MAY 21
Ye Are the Temple of God

The Lord rewarded me according to my righteousness: according to the cleanness of my hands hath he recompensed me.

2 SAMUEL 22:21

See also Pss. 18:24; 51:10; 1 Cor. 3:16–17; 2 Cor. 6:16.

"Know ye not that your body is the temple of the Holy Ghost which is in you, which ye have of God, and ye are not your own? . . . therefore glorify God in your body, and in your spirit, which are God's." If we can get a person to think what those words mean, then we can begin to understand the significance of the word of the renounced psychologist, MacDougall, from whom I have previously quoted, "The first thing to be done to help a man to moral regeneration is to restore, if possible, his self-respect." How better may that self-respect be restored than to help him so fully understand the answer to that question, "Who am I?"

(Harold B. Lee, *Stand Ye in Holy Places* [Salt Lake City: Deseret Book, 1974], 12.)

156

MAY 22
Power of Example

And he said unto them, Why do ye such things? for I hear of your evil dealings by all this people. Nay, my sons; for it is no good report that I hear: ye make the Lord's people to transgress.

1 Samuel 2:23–24

See also Prov. 4:18; John 13:15; Alma 17:11; 3 Ne. 12:16.

How much more beautiful would be the world and the society in which we live if every father looked upon his children as the most precious of his assets, if he led them by the power of his example in kindness and love, and if in times of stress he blessed them by the authority of the holy priesthood; and if every mother regarded her children as the jewels of her life, as gifts from the God of heaven who is their Eternal Father, and brought them up with true affection in the wisdom and admonition of the Lord.

(Gordon B. Hinckley, *Teachings of Gordon B. Hinckley* [Salt Lake City: Deseret Book, 1997], 419.)

MAY 23
Honor God and He Will Honor You

Wherefore the Lord God of Israel saith, I said indeed that thy house, and the house of thy father, should walk before me for ever: but now the Lord saith, Be it far from me; for them that honour me I will honour, and they that despise me shall be lightly esteemed.

1 SAMUEL 2:30

See also Ex. 20:6; 2 Ne. 1:9; D&C 76:5.

If we will honor God and keep his commandments and live as we should, no matter where the storms may strike, the winds may blow, and the lightnings may flash, we will be as the children of God always have been when they have kept his commandments: we will be under the protecting hand of him who is all-powerful.

(George Albert Smith, *The Teachings of George Albert Smith* [Salt Lake City: Bookcraft, 1996], 5.)

MAY 24
Teach Youth the Way of the Lord

Therefore shall ye lay up these my words in your heart and in your soul, . . .

And ye shall teach them your children, speaking of them when thou sittest in thine house, and when thou walkest by the way, when thou liest down, and when thou risest up. . . .

That your days may be multiplied, and the days of your children, in the land which the Lord sware unto your fathers to give them, as the days of heaven upon the earth.

DEUTERONOMY 11:18–19, 21

See also Deut. 6:7; Mosiah 4:14–15; Moses 6:57–58.

In this age of permissive parents and soft permissive educational leaders, it is happening to tens of thousands of our youth. Why? Because these choice young people have not been properly alerted and informed by parents and teachers who are recreant to the greatest God-given trust, and because many students do not seem to appreciate their priceless heritage and other rich blessings.

(Ezra Taft Benson, *The Teachings of Ezra Taft Benson* [Salt Lake City: Bookcraft, 1988], 307.)

MAY 25
Chastening

He that spareth his rod hateth his son: but he that loveth him chasteneth him betimes.

PROVERBS 13:24

See also Job 5:17; Prov. 3:11; 10:17; 2 Tim. 3:16.

In order that the young, vigorous, and inquiring minds of youth in all ages might have a standard and an unfailing guide by which to measure all learning and thus be able to sift the golden kernels of truth from the chaff of delusion and untruth, we have had the scriptures from the beginning that were given "by inspiration of God, and [are] profitable for doctrine, for reproof, for correction, for instruction in righteousness: that the man of God may be perfect, throughly furnished unto all good works."

(Harold B. Lee, *The Teachings of Harold B. Lee* [Salt Lake City: Bookcraft, 1996], 150.)

MAY 26
The Lord Will Dwell Among His People

And I will dwell among the children of Israel, and will be their God.

And they shall know that I am the Lord their God, that brought them forth out of the land of Egypt, that I may dwell among them: I am the Lord their God.

EXODUS 29:45–46

See also Ex. 19:17; Num. 14:14; 3 Ne. 20:1; D&C 88:126.

We believe that it is necessary for man to be placed in communication with God; that he should have revelation from him, and that unless he is placed under the influences of the inspiration of the Holy Spirit, he can know nothing about the things of God. . . . Not revelation in former times, but present and immediate revelation, which shall lead and guide those who possess it in all the paths of life here, and to eternal life hereafter. A good many people, and those professing Christians, will sneer a good deal at the idea of present revelation. Whoever heard of true religion without communication with God?

(John Taylor, *The Gospel Kingdom: Selections from the Writings and Discourses of John Taylor* [Salt Lake City: Improvement Era, 1941], 35.)

And the Lord came, and stood, and called as at other times, Samuel, Samuel. Then Samuel answered, Speak; for thy servant heareth.

1 SAMUEL 3:10

See also Alma 37:37; D&C 6:11; 88:63–64.

If one rises from his knees having merely said words, he should fall back on his knees and remain there until he has established communication with the Lord who is very anxious to bless, but having given man his free agency, will not force himself upon that man.

(Spencer W. Kimball, *The Teachings of Spencer W. Kimball*, [Salt Lake City: Bookcraft, 1982], 124.)

MAY 28
Your Decisions Reflect Your Values

And the Lord said unto Samuel, Hearken unto the voice of the people in all that they say unto thee: for they have not rejected thee, but they have rejected me, that I should not reign over them.

According to all the works which they have done since the day that I brought them up out of Egypt even unto this day, wherewith they have forsaken me, and served other gods, so do they also unto thee.

Now therefore hearken unto their voice: howbeit yet protest solemnly unto them, and shew them the manner of the king that shall reign over them.

And Samuel told all the words of the Lord unto the people that asked of him a king.

1 SAMUEL 8:7–10

See also Deut. 30:19; Josh. 24:15; 2 Ne. 2:27; Abr. 3:25.

Having decided to keep control of the course of your life you must make decisions daily. You must choose, elect, decide. Each decision implies a knowledge of values.

(Hugh B. Brown, *The Eternal Quest* [Salt Lake City: Bookcraft, 1956], 364.)

MAY 29
Seek and Follow the Prophets

Then said Saul to his servant, Well said; come, let us go. So they went unto the city where the man of God was.

1 Samuel 9:10

See also Amos 3:7; 3 Ne. 28:34–35; D&C 1:38; 21:1–6.

Next, let us nurture the seed of faith that gives us the courage to follow the prophets. Our prophet today is the Lord's spokesman to mankind at this time. We need the wisdom and the courage to accept his inspired counsel with gratitude and conform our lives to it, because "whether by mine own voice or by the voice of my servants, it is the same." The revelations given to Joseph Smith on the day the Church was organized apply to Latter-day Saints today: "The church . . . shalt give heed unto all his [the Prophet's] words and commandments which he shall give unto you as he receiveth them, . . . for his word ye shall receive, as if from mine own mouth, in all patience and faith."

(Joseph B. Wirthlin, *Finding Peace in Our Lives* [Salt Lake City: Deseret Book, 1995], 215–16.)

MAY 30
Humility

And Saul answered and said, Am not I a Benjamite, of the smallest of the tribes of Israel? and my family the least of all the families of the tribe of Benjamin? wherefore then speakest thou so to me?

1 Samuel 9:21

See also 2 Chr. 7:14; Job 22:29; Prov. 15:33; Mosiah 4:11.

There is danger that we may permit our own inclinations and desires to influence us and we may be stubborn enough and lack the essential humility, so that the Holy Ghost cannot break through the shell with which we surround ourselves. Therefore, we should seek for humility in the spirit of prayer and obedience so that we may always be subject to the teachings of the Spirit of the Lord.

(Joseph Fielding Smith, *Church History and Modern Revelation* [Salt Lake City: The Church of Jesus Christ of Latter-day Saints, 1946–1949], 2:29–30.)

MAY 31
Strength in the Lord

Whom have I in heaven but thee? and there is none upon earth that I desire beside thee.

My flesh and my heart faileth: but God is the strength of my heart, and my portion for ever.

Psalm 73:25–26

See also Ex. 15:2; 2 Sam. 22:23; Alma 26:12.

"The Lord is the strength of my life; of whom shall I be afraid? Though an host should encamp against me, my heart shall not fear." In their rendition of this heroic poem, the Jews add to the last line, "For thou art with me."

The assembled throng dared not interfere with Abinadi, nor did they molest him, for they saw in his countenance, the Spirit of God, making it bright like "Rays of Living Light."

(George Reynolds and Janne M. Sjodahl, *Commentary on the Book of Mormon* [Salt Lake City: Deseret Book, 1955–1961], 2:139.)

UNE

*God did send me before you to
preserve life.*

—GENESIS 45:5

JUNE 1
Trust in the Lord

Trust in the Lord with all thine heart; and lean not unto thine own understanding.

In all thy ways acknowledge him, and he shall direct thy paths.

PROVERBS 3:5–6

See also 2 Sam. 22:3; Ps. 62:8; Prov. 16:20; 2 Ne. 4:19, 34.

Put your trust in the Lord, have faith, and it will work out. The Lord never gives a commandment without providing the means to accomplish it.

(Ezra Taft Benson, *Come, Listen to a Prophet's Voice* [Salt Lake City: Deseret Book, 1990], 53.)

JUNE 2

Obedience Is Greater than Sacrifice

~~~~~~~~~~~~~

And Samuel said, Hath the Lord as great delight in burnt offerings and sacrifices, as in obeying the voice of the Lord? Behold, to obey is better than sacrifice, and to hearken than the fat of rams.

1 SAMUEL 15:22

See also Deut. 30:20; 2 Ne. 33:15; D&C 130:19–21.

The first law of heaven is obedience, and every dispensation of truth has required such. Certainly the fulness of the gospel requires commandment-keeping every bit as much as the lesser law of Moses, so notwithstanding their greater understanding of the gospel, the Nephite prophets and parents were determined to "keep the law because of the commandments" if only out of sheer loyalty to the principles of obedience and integrity.

(Jeffrey R. Holland, *Christ and the New Covenant: The Messianic Message of the Book of Mormon* [Salt Lake City: Deseret Book, 1997], 139–40.)

JUNE 3
Forgiveness

For thou, Lord, art good, and ready to forgive; and plenteous in mercy unto all them that call upon thee.

PSALM 86:5

See also Lev. 4:20; Matt. 6:14–15; Luke 6:37; Enos 1:5.

Don't ever feel that you can't be forgiven. Our Father in Heaven loves you. He is your Father. He is your Heavenly Parent. He has great concern for you. He reaches out to you in love and in forgiveness. . . . The Lord has said, "I the Lord will forgive whom I will forgive, but of you it is required to forgive all men." That is a mandate to us. Our Father in Heaven will take care of the forgiveness.

(Gordon B. Hinckley, *Teachings of Gordon B. Hinckley* [Salt Lake City: Deseret Book, 1997], 231.)

JUNE 4

Recognize and Remember the Goodness of God

And the Lord passed by before him, and proclaimed, The Lord, The Lord God, merciful and gracious, longsuffering, and abundant in goodness and truth.

Exodus 34:6

See also Deut. 4:31; 5:10; 2 Chr. 30:9; Alma 32:22.

How can you and I remember, always, the goodness of God, that we can retain a remission of our sins? The Apostle John recorded what the Savior taught us of a gift of remembrance which comes through the gift of the Holy Ghost: "But the Comforter, which is the Holy Ghost, whom the Father will send in my name, he shall teach you all things, and bring all things to your remembrance, whatsoever I have said unto you."

The Holy Ghost brings back memories of what God has taught us. And one of the ways God teaches us is with his blessings; and so, if we choose to exercise faith, the Holy Ghost will bring God's kindnesses to our remembrance.

(Henry B. Eyring, *To Draw Closer to God: A Collection of Discourses* [Salt Lake City: Deseret Book, 1997], 77–78.)

JUNE 5
True Friendship

And it came to pass, when he had made an end of speaking unto Saul, that the soul of Jonathan was knit with the soul of David, and Jonathan loved him as his own soul.

Then Jonathan and David made a covenant, because he loved him as his own soul.

1 SAMUEL 18:1, 3

See also Prov. 17:17; 18:24.

When the Prophet Joseph Smith was suffering in Liberty Jail, he wrote of the balm he received from his friends. He said:

"Those who have not been enclosed in the walls of prison without cause . . . can have but little idea how sweet the voice of a friend is; one token of friendship from any source whatever awakens and calls into action every sympathetic feeling; . . . then the voice of inspiration steals along and whispers, . . . 'peace be unto thy soul.'"

Joseph recognized the role each of us plays in lifting, helping, and soothing so that the calamities of life can be stilled and the Lord's voice can be heard.

(Elaine L. Jack, "Relief Society: A Balm in Gilead," *Ensign*, Nov. 1995, 90.)

JUNE 6
Look to Strengthen Others

Strengthen ye the weak hands, and confirm the feeble knees.

Say to them that are of a fearful heart, Be strong, fear not: behold, your God will come with vengeance, even God with a recompence; he will come and save you.

ISAIAH 35:3–4

See also Luke 22:32; Mosiah 4:16; D&C 81:5; 108:7.

When we have a testimony, we are expected to use it for the benefit of others, as Peter was instructed: "When thou art converted, strengthen thy brethren."

All of us have so many, many opportunities to strengthen others. It may be our own brothers and sisters. It may be our friends. It may be a neighbor or a new acquaintance. It may even be our own parents. Now that's a great concept, isn't it—parents and youth strengthening one another.

(Harold B. Lee, *Stand Ye in Holy Places* [Salt Lake City: Deseret Book, 1974], 93–94.)

JUNE 7
Vengeance and Revenge

To me belongeth vengeance, and recompence; their foot shall slide in due time: for the day of their calamity is at hand, and the things that shall come upon them make haste.

DEUTERONOMY 32:35

See also Ps. 94:1; Morm. 3:15; D&C 97:22; 98:23.

The stake president and I gave the father and the daughters blessings of comfort, admonishing them to nourish feelings of forgiveness so that this evil deed done to their mother would not canker their souls. . . . I shall ever remember his gratitude for all our blessings and his plea to "bless those who are less fortunate than we are." Certainly there was to be loneliness and the continual wrestle to overcome vindictive feelings of revenge, but through it all was the pure love of Christ for "those who are less fortunate," and these feelings brought relief from pain and despair.

(Spencer J. Condie, *In Perfect Balance* [Salt Lake City: Bookcraft, 1993], 188.)

JUNE 8
Overcoming Jealousy

For jealousy is the rage of a man.

PROVERBS 6:34

See also Ps. 73:3; 106:16; Prov. 24:1; Matt. 5:44; Ether 9:7.

The more we try to cultivate the attributes of the Savior, the stronger we become in character and in spirituality. We should so live that we may be susceptible to the inspiration of the Holy Ghost and to his guidance. . . . The whole purpose of life is to bring under subjection the animal passions, proclivities, and tendencies, that we might realize the companionship always of God's Holy Spirit.

One chief purpose of life is to overcome evil tendencies, to govern our appetites, to control our passions—anger, hatred, jealousy, immorality. We have to overcome them, to conquer them, because God has said: "My spirit will not dwell in unclean tabernacles, nor will it always strive with man."

(David O. McKay, *Man May Know for Himself: Teachings of President David O. McKay* [Salt Lake City: Deseret Book, 1967], 17.)

JUNE 9

Conquering Hatred

Hatred stirreth up strifes: but love covereth all sins.

PROVERBS 10:12

See also Prov. 26:24; John 15:18; 1 Jn. 4:20; 3 Ne. 12:44.

I believe that our Father planted into our souls a special ingredient that, if used, will influence us toward heavenly things. . . . It may bring to us our greatest joy. It can help us overcome fear, peer pressure, hatred, selfishness, evil, and even sin.

This special ingredient, which is powerful beyond words, was explained by the Savior himself when he was asked which was the great commandment of the law. He said: "Thou shalt love the Lord thy God with all thy heart, and with all thy soul, and with all thy mind. This is the first and great commandment. And the second is like unto it, Thou shalt love thy neighbour as thyself. On these two commandments hang all the law and the prophets."

Love is this divine ingredient.

(David B. Haight, *A Light unto the World* [Salt Lake City: Deseret Book, 1997], 123–24.)

JUNE 10
Wisdom in All Things

Wisdom is the principal thing; therefore get wisdom: and with all thy getting get understanding.

PROVERBS 4:7

See also Prov. 8:11; James 1:5; Mosiah 2:17; D&C 136:32.

Worldly wisdom and knowledge gained by intellectual talents are available to all men. But the knowledge of God and his eternal laws—gospel knowledge, saving knowledge, the hidden wisdom that comes from on high, the wisdom of those to whom the wonders of eternity are an open book, divine wisdom—all these are gifts of the Spirit. "The things of God knoweth no man, but the Spirit of God."

Among the true saints are those endowed with divine knowledge and heavenly wisdom "that all may be taught to be wise and to have knowledge."

(Bruce R. McConkie, *A New Witness for the Articles of Faith* [Salt Lake City: Deseret Book, 1985], 372–73.)

JUNE 11

Love as the Lord Loveth

The Lord hath appeared of old unto me, saying, Yea, I have loved thee with an everlasting love: therefore with lovingkindness have I drawn thee.

JEREMIAH 31:3

See also Matt. 25:40; John 13:34–35; 1 Jn. 4:21.

This must be the foundation of our instruction: love of God and love for and service to others—neighbors, family, and all with whom we have association. That which we teach must be constantly gauged against these two standards established by the Lord. If we shall do so, this work will continue to roll forward.

(Gordon B. Hinckley, *Teachings of Gordon B. Hinckley* [Salt Lake City: Deseret Book, 1997], 316–17.)

JUNE 12

As a Man Thinketh

For as he thinketh in his heart, so is he.

PROVERBS 23:7

See also Ps. 119:15; Prov. 4:26; Matt. 15:18–20.

No principle of life was more constantly emphasized by the Great Teacher than the necessity of right thinking. To Him, the man was not what he appeared to be outwardly, nor what he professed to be by his words: what the man *thought* determined in all cases what the man *was*. No teacher emphasized more strongly than He the truth that 'as a man thinketh in his heart, so is he.' . . . Contentment, complacency, peace—all that makes life worth living—have their source in the mind of the individual. From the same source spring unrest, turbulence, misery—everything that leads to dissolution and death. . . . It is well for [every teacher and officer in the Church] to pause frequently and take stock of himself to ascertain 'what he is thinking about when he doesn't have to think,' for 'what he thinketh in his heart, so is he.'

(David O. McKay, "Developing Character," *Ensign,* Oct. 2001, 22.)

JUNE 13
Testimony of Jesus Christ

The law of the Lord is perfect, converting the soul: the testimony of the Lord is sure, making wise the simple.

PSALM 19:7

See also Job 19:25; Ps. 132:12; Acts 14:3; Alma 5:45–46.

Strive to build a personal testimony of Jesus Christ and the atonement. A study of the life of Christ and a testimony of his reality is something each of us should seek. As we come to understand his mission, and the atonement which he wrought, we will desire to live more like him. . . . When temptations come, as they surely will, an understanding of the Savior's agony in Gethsemane and his eventual death on the cross will be a reminder to you to avoid any activity that would cause the Savior more pain. Listen to his words, "For behold, I, God, have suffered these things for all, that they might not suffer if they would repent; But if they would not repent, they must suffer even as I."

(Howard W. Hunter, *The Teachings of Howard W. Hunter* [Salt Lake City: Bookcraft, 1997], 30–31.)

JUNE 14
Put on the Armor of God

Then said David to the Philistine, Thou comest to me with a sword, and with a spear, and with a shield: but I come to thee in the name of the Lord of hosts, the God of the armies of Israel, whom thou hast defied.

1 SAMUEL 17:45

See also Dan. 6:16, 22; 2 Cor. 6:7: Eph. 6:11.

The loins were to be "girt about with truth." . . . "The breastplate of righteousness," which would be placed over the heart. . . . The next part to be armored was the feet, which were to be "shod with the preparation of the gospel of peace," the feet denoting one's course in life. . . . And, finally, the warrior was to have a "helmet of salvation," which of course speaks of the intellect.

(Harold B. Lee, *The Teachings of Harold B. Lee* [Salt Lake City: Bookcraft, 1996], 168.)

JUNE 15
Chastity

Thou shalt not commit adultery.

EXODUS 20:14

See also Prov. 6:25; 12:4; James 1:14; Jacob 2:28.

When we obey the law of chastity and keep ourselves morally clean, we will experience the blessings of increased love and peace, greater trust and respect for our marital partners, deeper commitment to each other, and therefore a deep and significant sense of joy and happiness.

"We must not be misled into thinking these sins are minor or that consequences are not that serious."

President Thomas S. Monson added these words of wise counsel: "Because sexual intimacy is so sacred, the Lord requires self-control and purity before marriage, as well as full fidelity after marriage. In dating, treat your date with respect, and expect your date to show that same respect for you. Tears inevitably follow transgression. Men, take care not to make women weep, for God counts their tears."

(Alexander B. Morrison, *Zion: A Light in the Darkness* [Salt Lake City: Deseret Book, 1997], 81.)

JUNE 16
Seek Not to Cover Your Sins

Woe to the rebellious children, saith the Lord, that take counsel, but not of me; and that cover with a covering, but not of my spirit, that they may add sin to sin.

ISAIAH 30:1

See also Neh. 4:5; D&C 121:37.

Strange as it is, there are those who deliberately cultivate a sense of fundamental hopelessness and who therein seek to justify, to cover, and to continue in their sins. Just as too much physical idleness can induce lust, so intellectual slackness provides the dusk in which wrong deeds are considered, rationalized, and then encouraged.

(Neal A. Maxwell, *Even As I Am* [Salt Lake City: Deseret Book, 1982], 80.)

JUNE 17
Seek Forgiveness

Have mercy upon me, O God, according to thy lovingkindness: according unto the multitude of thy tender mercies blot out my transgressions.

Wash me throughly from mine iniquity, and cleanse me from my sin.

PSALM 51:1–2

See also Ex. 34:9; Ps. 32:5; Luke 5:20; 3 Ne. 13:14.

If sin has deprived us of peace within, we can repent and seek forgiveness. The Lord said that he "cannot look upon sin with the least degree of allowance; nevertheless, he that repents and does the commandments of the Lord shall be forgiven." President Spencer W. Kimball wrote: "The essence of the miracle of forgiveness is that it brings peace to the previously anxious, restless, frustrated, perhaps tormented soul. In a world of turmoil and contention this is indeed a priceless gift."

(Joseph B. Wirthlin, *Finding Peace in Our Lives* [Salt Lake City: Deseret Book, 1995], 9–10.)

JUNE 18

Obedience to the Lord

And Abraham rose up early in the morning, and saddled his ass, and took two of his young men with him, and Isaac his son, and clave the wood for the burnt offering, and rose up, and went unto the place of which God had told him . . .

And Abraham took the wood of the burnt offering, and laid it upon Isaac his son; and he took the fire in his hand, and a knife; and they went both of them together.

GENESIS 22:3, 6

See also Isa. 1:19; Matt. 7:21; D&C 82:10; Abr. 3:25.

Our ability to hear the voice of the Spirit is dependent upon our willingness to keep the commandments, for "when we obtain any blessing from God, it is by obedience to that law upon which it is predicated." If we want to experience the inexpressible joy of gospel living and feel of Christ's atoning mercies, obedience to all, and not just a select few, of God's commandments is the only way. . . .

Will you contemplate the blessings that await your obedience in this life and throughout eternity?

(Mary Ellen Smoot, "We Are Instruments in the Hands of God," *Ensign,* Nov. 2000, 90–92.)

JUNE 19
Gratitude for the Creation

O Lord, how manifold are thy works! in wisdom hast thou made them all: the earth is full of thy riches.

PSALM 104:24

See also Ps. 19:1; Eph. 5:20; D&C 88:13.

Without the Creation, we would not exist. The earth would not be; there would be no universe. There would be nothing if it were not for God, our Heavenly Father, by whom all things originated. Consequently, we are in a position in which we ought to give praise, glory, adoration, thanksgiving, and worship to him for the creation of all things, for our existence, and for the very being that we possess. Without God, we are not. He deserves all the worship that we are able to give him. Our problem is to learn how to worship and what we should do to repay him for the great, glorious, and infinite fact of existence and creation.

(Bruce R. McConkie, *Sermons and Writings of Bruce R. McConkie* [Salt Lake City: Bookcraft, 1998], 375.)

JUNE 20
Gratitude for the Word of God

Remember the word unto thy servant, upon which thou hast caused me to hope.

This is my comfort in my affliction: for thy word hath quickened me. . . .

Thy statutes have been my songs in the house of my pilgrimage.

PSALM 119:49–50, 54

See also Ps. 19:7–8; Hel. 3:29; D&C 84:43–46.

I am grateful for emphasis on reading the scriptures. I hope that for you this will become something far more enjoyable than a duty; that, rather, it will become a love affair with the word of God. I promise you that as you read, your minds will be enlightened and your spirits will be lifted. At first it may seem tedious, but that will change into a wondrous experience with thoughts and words of things divine.

(Gordon B. Hinckley, *Teachings of Gordon B. Hinckley* [Salt Lake City: Deseret Book, 1997], 573–74.)

Offer unto God thanksgiving; and pay thy vows unto the most High.

PSALM 50:14

See also Pss. 95:2; 100:4; 1 Thes. 2:13; Mosiah 26:39.

I feel that of all people under heaven we ought to be the most grateful to our God; and that we ought to remember to keep our covenants, and humble ourselves before him, and labor with all our hearts to discharge faithfully the responsibilities which devolve upon us, and the duties which are required at our hands. For we can afford to do anything which God requires of us; but none of us can afford to do wrong. It would cost far more than this world with all its wealth is worth for the Latter-day Saints to do wrong and come under the disfavor of Almighty God.

(Wilford Woodruff, *The Discourses of Wilford Woodruff* [Salt Lake City: Bookcraft, 1969], 122.)

Mercy of God

For the Lord your God is gracious and merciful, and will not turn away his face from you, if ye return unto him.

2 CHRONICLES 30:9

See also Neh. 9:31; Ether 11:8; D&C 29:1.

All individuals will receive "according to their works, according to the desire of their hearts." The justice and mercy of God will have combined so that by then all inhabitants of the earth will have heard the gospel of Jesus Christ sufficiently to be fully accountable for it. . . . Each individual will have had full opportunity to forge his decision, to give his real desires full expression. We will receive what we really chose, and none can or will question the justice or mercy of God.

(Neal A. Maxwell, *Things As They Really Are* [Salt Lake City: Deseret Book, 1978], 112–13.)

JUNE 23
Trust in the Lord

And they that know thy name will put their trust in thee: for thou, Lord, hast not forsaken them that seek thee.

See also Pss. 16:1; 22:4; 25:20; 118:8; 125:1.

I am anchored by the powerful words of President Gordon B. Hinckley: "We have nothing to fear. God is at the helm . . . he will shower down blessings upon those who walk in obedience to his commandments." I am convinced that now more than ever before we must be thus reassured. We can have unwavering, unquestionable, undeniable trust in our Father in Heaven.

(Ardeth Greene Kapp, *Rejoice! His Promises Are Sure* [Salt Lake City: Deseret Book, 1997], 3.)

JUNE 24
The House of the Lord

I was glad when they said unto me, Let us go into the house of the Lord. . . .

Because of the house of the Lord our God I will seek thy good.

PSALM 122:1, 9

See also Ex. 40:34; Isa. 2:3; Ezek. 44:11; D&C 97:15; 110:7.

The temple ordinances are so imbued with symbolic meaning as to provide a lifetime of productive contemplation and learning. Ponder each word and activity in the temple. Study how they interrelate. As you ponder the significance of those matters, think of them in light of your relationship to the Savior and His to our Father in Heaven. Contemplate how the understanding you receive enhances your earth life by giving proper emphasis on things which are critically important. . . . Do these things with a prayer in your heart that the Holy Spirit will enhance your understanding and enrich your life. Those worthy prayers will be answered.

(Richard G. Scott, "Receive the Temple Blessings," *Ensign,* May 1999, 27.)

Care for Others

And when ye reap the harvest of your land, thou shalt not wholly reap the corners of thy field, neither shalt thou gather the gleanings of thy harvest. . . . Neither shalt thou gather every grape of thy vineyard; thou shalt leave them for the poor and stranger: I am the Lord your God.

LEVITICUS 19:9–10

See also Ps. 142:4; Isa. 1:17; Gal. 6:2; Mosiah 18:8–9.

At the end of the day, our belief in Christ will best be reflected to others by the extent to which we practice what we preach. Elder Neal A. Maxwell has reminded us: "Overall, the perception of us as a Church and people will improve in direct proportion to the degree to which we mirror the Master in our lives. No media effort can do as much good—over the sweep of time—as can *believing, behaving,* and *serving* members of the Church! The eloquence of such examples will be felt and seen in any culture or community."

(Alexander B. Morrison, *Feed My Sheep: Leadership Ideas for Latter-day Shepherds* [Salt Lake City: Deseret Book, 1992], 134.)

JUNE 26
An Understanding Heart

Give therefore thy servant an understanding heart to judge thy people, that I may discern between good and bad.

1 KINGS 3:9

See also Ezra 7:10; Matt. 5:8; D&C 64:34.

Having a change of heart at one time in our lives is insufficient to give us an understanding heart today. Helping and understanding a person years ago do not fill us with the love of God today. Christlike love must be continuous and contemporary. . . . I pray that God will give each of us the courage and desire to strive for a pure heart, a willing heart, an understanding and loving heart.

(Marvin J. Ashton, *The Measure of Our Hearts* [Salt Lake City: Deseret Book, 1991], 7.)

JUNE 27
Wisdom of God

For my thoughts are not your thoughts, neither are your ways my ways, saith the Lord.

For as the heavens are higher than the earth, so are my ways higher than your ways, and my thoughts than your thoughts.

ISAIAH 55:8–9
See also Job 36:5; Ps. 136:5; D&C 76:2.

But all is managed in the wisdom of God and in ways that we mortals must simply trust, because of our faith in the omniscient Lord. It is significant, in this as well as in many other respects, that the vision of those in the celestial kingdom (seen by the Prophet Joseph Smith) was of those "who overcome by faith"—*not* because while in mortality they had it all figured out, being perpetually able to give a logical, precise explanation for everything.

(Neal A. Maxwell, *All These Things Shall Give Thee Experience* [Salt Lake City: Deseret Book, 1979], 34–35.)

JUNE 28
Motives Make the Difference

And God said unto him, Because thou hast asked this thing, and hast not asked for thyself long life; neither hast asked riches for thyself, nor hast asked the life of thine enemies; but hast asked for thyself understanding to discern judgment;

Behold, I have done according to thy words: lo, I have given thee a wise and an understanding heart; so that there was none like thee before thee, neither after thee shall any arise like unto thee.

1 KINGS 3:11–12

See also Prov. 16:3; 23:7; Moro. 7:6; D&C 88:67.

We must not only *do* what is right. We must act for the right reasons. The modern term is *good motive*. The scriptures often signify this appropriate mental attitude with the words *full purpose of heart or real intent.*

The scriptures make clear that God understands our motives and will judge our actions accordingly. If we do not act for the right reasons, our acts will not be counted for righteousness.

(Dallin H. Oaks, *Pure in Heart* [Salt Lake City: Bookcraft, 1988], 15.)

JUNE 29
Gifts of the Spirit

Then Samuel took the horn of oil, and anointed him in the midst of his brethren: and the Spirit of the Lord came upon David from that day forward. So Samuel rose up, and went to Ramah.

1 SAMUEL 16:13

See also Ex. 31:3; Num.11:25; 1 Sam. 10:6; Moro. 10:4–25.

What did Nephi say was the basis for receiving the Holy Ghost? Faith in the Lord Jesus Christ. . . . He said the Holy Ghost is "the gift of God unto all those who diligently seek him." Diligently surely means regularly. And it surely means pondering and praying. And the praying will surely include a fervent pleading to know the truth. Anything less would hardly be diligent. And anything less will not be enough for you and for me.

(Henry B. Eyring, *To Draw Closer to God: A Collection of Discourses* [Salt Lake City: Deseret Book, 1997], 118.)

JUNE 30
Righteous and Wise Judgment

Ye shall do no unrighteousness in judgment: thou shalt not respect the person of the poor, nor honour the person of the mighty: but in righteousness shalt thou judge thy neighbour.

LEVITICUS 19:15

See also Deut. 16:19; John 7:24; Alma 41:14; Ether 7:11.

The only safe way for us to do, as individuals, is to live so humbly, so righteously and so faithfully before God that we may possess his Spirit to that extent that we shall be able to judge righteously, and discern between truth and error, between right and wrong.

(Joseph F. Smith, *Gospel Doctrine: Selections from the Sermons and Writings of Joseph F. Smith* [Salt Lake City: Deseret Book, 1939], 45.)

 JULY

Wither thou goest, I will go;
and where thou lodgest, I will
lodge . . .

—RUTH 1:16

JULY 1
Spiritual Wealth

They that trust in their wealth, and boast themselves in the multitude of their riches;

None of them can by any means redeem his brother, nor give to God a ransom for him.

PSALM 49:6–7

See also Prov. 23:4; Eccl. 5:10; Jacob 2:18–19; Alma 39:14.

How powerful a role our true desires play in our lives! Desire both initiates our actions and sustains—for good or evil. If we desire wealth or power, these will tend to be the moving causes of our actions. If instead we desire spiritual things and are obedient, the promised blessings will come to us. . . . Clearly, those who discount spiritual things and do not really desire and seek those things will not receive them.

(Neal A. Maxwell, *Not My Will, But Thine* [Salt Lake City: Bookcraft, 1998], 89.)

JULY 2

A Heart Perfect with the Lord

Let your heart therefore be perfect with the Lord our God, to walk in his statutes, and to keep his commandments, as at this day.

1 KINGS 8:61

See also 1 Chron. 29:9; Acts 11:23; Hel. 3:35; Morm. 9:27.

The scriptures say that when we desire righteousness our "heart is right" with God. The Psalmist condemned the people of ancient Israel because "their heart was not right with [God]." When King Solomon blessed the people at the dedication of the temple, he concluded with these words: "Let your heart therefore be perfect with the Lord our God, to walk in his statutes, and to keep his commandments, as at this day."

Our heart is right or perfect with God when we desire what God desires.

(Dallin H. Oaks, *Pure in Heart* [Salt Lake City: Bookcraft, 1988], 4.)

JULY 3
Example

There was a man in the land of Uz, whose name was Job; and that man was perfect and upright, and one that feared God, and eschewed evil.

JOB 1:1

See also Prov. 4:18; 29:2; Isa. 3:12; Jarom 1:7; Mosiah 23:14.

Christ taught us to be *other-centered*. It is not enough for us to live the gospel inwardly; we need to be shining examples to all with whom we come in contact. In this sense, it's not only what we *are* that's important: what others think of us is *also* important. In order to be truly effective as missionaries, we need to be known for our good qualities, to have an unspotted reputation in all things.

I would like, for example, to be known for my dependability—for being honest and upright in all my dealings. . . . I would like to be known as one who is trustworthy and as one whose loyalty is unquestionable. I would like to be known as one who keeps the commandments and one who is fully committed in helping to build the kingdom of God.

(O. Leslie Stone, "The Importance of Reputation," *Ensign,* Nov. 1975, 40.)

JULY 4
Proclaim Liberty

And ye shall hallow the fiftieth year, and proclaim liberty throughout all the land unto all the inhabitants thereof: it shall be a jubile unto you; and ye shall return every man unto his possession, and ye shall return every man unto his family.

LEVITICUS 25:10

See also Isa. 58:6; 61:1; Jer. 34:8; Alma 61:14–15; D&C 134:4–5.

It seems logical that if we are to preserve the freedom and liberty vouchsafed to us by our pioneer fathers we must pursue likewise their lofty ideals.

(Harold B. Lee, *Decisions for Successful Living* [Salt Lake City: Deseret Book, 1973], 6.)

JULY 5
Serve God

And now, Israel, what doth the Lord thy God require of thee, but to fear the Lord thy God, to walk in all his ways, and to love him, and to serve the Lord thy God with all thy heart and with all thy soul.

DEUTERONOMY 10:12

See also Deut. 6:13; 11:13–14; Mosiah 8:18; D&C 4:2.

In a real sense, therefore, the greatest leaders do not see themselves as such. They seek only to serve, with no desire for self-aggrandizement or acclaim. They see themselves as the Lord's servants, on His errand, acting as His agents, imbued with a deep sense of responsibility to further His interests rather than their own. . . . Over what, then, are the Lord's servant-leaders to be stewards? The answer is simple: over *all* that He has given them—every material blessing, every talent, every responsibility.

(Alexander B. Morrison, *Feed My Sheep: Leadership Ideas for Latter-day Shepherds* [Salt Lake City: Deseret Book, 1992], 20–21.)

JULY 6
A Leader Must Teach

And thou shalt teach them ordinances and laws,
and shalt shew them the way wherein they must walk,
and the work that they must do.

EXODUS 18:20

See also Lev. 10:11; Deut. 24:8; Mal. 2:7; Alma 17:11.

The central activity of leadership is teaching—
first by example, second by precept. After that,
leaders become a source of help as their empowered
stewards assume the responsibility and exercise the
initiative to do whatever is necessary, consistent with
the principles taught, to fulfill the shared vision.

The most advanced, universal, and practical
leadership philosophy ever put forth was given in
this simple statement by the Prophet Joseph Smith:
"I teach the people correct principles and they govern
themselves."

(M. Russell Ballard, *Counseling with Our Councils: Learning
to Minister Together in the Church and in the Family* [Salt Lake
City: Deseret Book, 1997], 58.)

JULY 7

Leaders Care for the Individual

Son of man, prophesy against the shepherds of Israel, prophesy, and say unto them, Thus saith the Lord God unto the shepherds; Woe be to the shepherds of Israel that do feed themselves! should not the shepherds feed the flocks?

EZEKIEL 34:2

See also Ps. 142:4; Ezek. 33:7; Matt. 25:40; 3 Ne. 17:21.

If each of us reflects upon failure experiences in leadership roles, large or small, it is probable that most of the things we would like to do again are things that relate directly to failures in our relationship with other people in the areas of candor and openness. We may say of our failure experience in a particular leadership role that we should have prepared better agenda, we should have given people more clear-cut job descriptions, etc., but it is much more likely that our failures are the failures in which we were unwilling to confront our associates with their weaknesses, or the failures in which we were not praise-giving or because we kept others at arm's length and would not let them come too close to us.

(Neal A. Maxwell, *A More Excellent Way: Essays on Leadership for Latter-day Saints* [Salt Lake City: Deseret Book], 95.)

JULY 8
Leaders Delegate Wisely

And let them judge the people at all seasons: and it shall be, that every great matter they shall bring unto thee, but every small matter they shall judge: so shall it be easier for thyself, and they shall bear the burden with thee.

EXODUS 18:22

See also Ex. 18:25; Num. 11:16–17; Deut. 1:13; 1 Kgs. 4:7.

One purpose of Church callings is to benefit individual members by letting them do the work of the Church. Responsibility and authority are distributed locally. Leaders delegate to officers and teachers the responsibility of conceiving, planning, preparing, and executing the activities pertinent to their callings. This decentralized organization encourages initiative and personal growth among members of local wards and stakes. Through service, members learn their responsibility and their capacity, enlarge their understanding, and increase their commitment to the gospel.

(Brian L. Pitcher, *Encyclopedia of Mormonism* [New York: Macmillan, 1992], 249.)

JULY 9
Lead with Love

The statutes of the Lord are right, rejoicing the heart: the commandment of the Lord is pure, enlightening the eyes.

PSALM 19:8

See also Ps. 18:28; Ezek. 34:2; John 13:34–35; 1 Jn. 4:7.

The successful leader leads with love. You never find the successful leader scolding nor giving vent to verbal tongue lashing. Rather, he follows the counsel of President George Albert Smith, who said, "It does not pay to scold. I believe you can get people to do anything (if you can get them to do it at all) by loving them into doing it." Think back to that teacher who influenced you most, and honestly ask yourself, "Did that teacher love me and my classmates, or did she scold us?" You know the answer. Where love prevails in a class, discipline problems vanish.

(Thomas S. Monson, *Be Your Best Self* [Salt Lake City: Deseret Book, 1979], 117.)

JULY 10
Worship and Glorify God

O come, let us worship and bow down: let us kneel before the Lord our maker.

PSALM 95:6

See also Deut. 6:13; 10:12; Ps. 99:9; 1 Cor. 10:31.

We should try to ascertain how we should spend the money and the information that God has given us. The answer is simple—for the glory of God. Our eye should be single to the glory of God. That is what we have left the other life for and come into this. We should seek to promote the interests of the Most High God, and to feel as Jesus felt, "I can of mine own self do nothing." Inasmuch as we act today and tomorrow, this week and next week, in the interest of God, and have our eye single to His glory, there can be no failure.

(Lorenzo Snow, *The Teachings of Lorenzo Snow* [Salt Lake City: Bookcraft, 1984], 107–08.)

JULY 11
Knowledge and Wisdom

The heart of the prudent getteth knowledge; and
the ear of the wise seeketh knowledge.

PROVERBS 18:15

See also Prov. 2:5; Isa. 33:6; Dan. 2:21; 2 Ne. 9:28–29.

In the use of knowledge Peter suggests the balance wheel of TEMPERANCE, because knowledge
is power and power can be dangerous. Much of the
world today is dominated by wilful, godless men
who, through technical knowledge, have the power
to destroy the world. Knowledge alone will not insure
salvation. While it is true that we are saved no faster
than we gain knowledge, it must be used with wisdom and develop into intelligence.

(Hugh B. Brown, *The Abundant Life* [Salt Lake City:
Bookcraft, 1965], 185.)

JULY 12
The Lord Blesses Us through Others

For the poor shall never cease out of the land: therefore I command thee, saying, Thou shalt open thine hand wide unto thy brother, to thy poor, and to thy needy, in thy land.

DEUTERONOMY 15:11

See also Deut. 10:12; 1 Kgs. 12:7; Mosiah 2:17; 8:18; 18:8–9.

History shows that there have been a number of people who have learned this great secret, that when service is freely given it becomes sweet. In going the second mile, these people honor our Heavenly Father by honoring themselves and honoring others.

Those who go the second mile are often blessed with another rare and unique gift—they discover the divine in others. When we consider that every soul who walks the earth may become like our spiritual Father in Heaven, it should humble us in the presence of any human soul.

(Vaughn J. Featherstone, "Secret of the Second Mile," *New Era,* May 1990, 4.)

JULY 13
Sabbath Day

Remember the sabbath day, to keep it holy.

Exodus 20:8

See also Gen. 2:3; Deut. 5:12; Mark 2:27; Mosiah 18:23.

Where is the line as to what is acceptable and unacceptable on the Sabbath? . . . While these guidelines are contained in the scriptures and in the words of the modern prophets, they must also be written in our hearts and governed by our consciences. Brigham Young said of the faithful that "The spirit of their religion leaks out of their hearts." It is quite unlikely that there will be any serious violation of Sabbath worship if we come humbly before the Lord and offer him all our heart, our soul, and our mind.

(James E. Faust, *Finding Light in a Dark World* [Salt Lake City: Deseret Book, 1995], 115.)

JULY 14
Serve the Lord

Thou shalt fear the Lord thy God, and serve him.

DEUTERONOMY 6:13

See also Matt. 6:24; Moses 1:15.

For "their hearts are upon their treasures; wherefore, their treasure is their God. And behold, their treasure shall perish with them also." Why does Jacob make this number one in his explicit list of offenses against God? Because it is the number-one device among the enticings of "that cunning one," who knows that riches are his most effective weapon in leading men astray. You must choose between being at one with God or with Mammon, not both; the one promises everything in this world for money, the other a place in the kingdom after you have "endured the crosses of the world, and despised the shame of it."

(Hugh Nibley, *Approaching Zion* [Salt Lake City and Provo: Deseret Book, Foundation for Ancient Research and Mormon Studies, 1989], 592–93.)

JULY 15
Peace

The Lord will give strength unto his people; the Lord will bless his people with peace.

PSALM 29:11

See also Pss. 34:14; 37:37; Isa. 32:17; John 14:27; Rom. 8:6.

Peace is not a purchase away. Peace is not when the final installment is paid. Peace is not when marriage comes nor when all the children are enrolled in school. Peace is not when the last child returns from the mission field. Peace is not when an inheritance is received. Peace is not when the scars of death start to heal.

True peace must not be dependent upon conditions or happenings. Peace must stem from an inward contentment built upon trust, faith, and goodwill toward God, others, and self. It must be constantly nurtured by the individual who is soundly anchored to the gospel of Jesus Christ. Only then can a person realize that the trials and tribulations of daily life are less important than God's total goodness.

Lasting peace is an eternal personal quest. Peace does come from obedience to the law. Peace comes to those who develop character and trust.

(Marvin J. Ashton, *Be of Good Cheer* [Salt Lake City: Deseret Book, 1987], 89.)

JULY 16
The Prophet Speaks for the Lord

Since the day that your fathers came forth out of the land of Egypt unto this day I have even sent unto you all my servants the prophets, daily rising up early and sending them.

JEREMIAH 7:25

See also Num. 12:6; 2 Kgs. 17:13; Amos 3:7; 3 Ne. 28:34–35.

President Benson taught that the prophet is the only man who speaks for the Lord, and that his words are more important than those of a deceased prophet.

(Sheri L. Dew, *Ezra Taft Benson: A Biography* [Salt Lake City: Deseret Book, 1987], 468–469.)

JULY 17
Power of God

Is any thing too hard for the Lord?

GENESIS 18:14

See also 2 Sam. 22:33; Jer. 32:17; Mark 10:27; 1 Ne. 7:12.

And again the Lord declared: "Seek not to declare my word, but first seek to obtain my word, and then shall your tongue be loosed; then, if you desire, you shall have my Spirit and my word, yea, the power of God unto the convincing of men."

The sequence of steps to possessing the power of God in teaching the gospel is to first seek to obtain the word, then to understand through the Spirit, and finally to have the power to convince.

(Ezra Taft Benson, *Come unto Christ* [Salt Lake City: Deseret Book, 1983], 92.)

JULY 18
Prophets Speak for the Lord

And he shall be thy spokesman unto the people:
and he shall be, even he shall be to thee instead of
a mouth, and thou shalt be to him instead of God.

Exodus 4:16

See also 2 Sam. 23:2; Jer. 1:9; Luke 1:68–70; 2 Pet. 3:2.

All prophets are spokesmen: true prophets speak
for God, and their words lead to life and salvation;
false prophets speak for the devil, and their words
lead to death and damnation.

(Bruce R. McConkie, *The Millennial Messiah: The Second
Coming of the Son of Man* [Salt Lake City: Deseret Book, 1982], 72.)

JULY 19
Sustaining the Prophet

And they rose early in the morning, and went forth into the wilderness of Tekoa: and as they went forth, Jehoshaphat stood and said, Hear me, O Judah, and ye inhabitants of Jerusalem; Believe in the Lord your God, so shall ye be established; believe his prophets, so shall ye prosper.

2 CHRONICLES 20:20

See also Ezek. 2:7; Heb. 13:17; D&C 26:2; 107:22.

When we sustain, it means we *do* something about our belief. Our testimony of the prophet turns into action when we sustain him. . . . In general conference in October 1994, Elder David B. Haight said: "When we sustain the President of the Church by our uplifted hand, it not only signifies that we acknowledge before God that he is the rightful possessor of all the priesthood keys; it means that we covenant with God that we will abide by the direction and the counsel that comes through His prophet. It is a solemn covenant."

(Janette Hales Beckham, "Sustaining the Living Prophets," *Ensign,* May 1996, 84.)

JULY 20
Priesthood Power Blesses Lives

But truly I am full of power by the spirit of the Lord, and of judgment, and of might, to declare unto Jacob his transgression, and to Israel his sin.

MICAH 3:8

See also Acts 19:11; 3 Ne. 7:17; D&C 84:19–20; 90:11.

I testify that the blessings of the priesthood, honored by fathers and husbands and revered by wives and children, can indeed cure the cancer that plagues our society. I plead with you, fathers, come home. Magnify your priesthood calling; bless your families through this sacred influence, and experience the rewards promised by our Father and God.

(James E. Faust, *Finding Light in a Dark World* [Salt Lake City: Deseret Book, 1995], 137.)

JULY 21
Miracles

Because all those men which have seen my glory, and my miracles, which I did in Egypt and in the wilderness, and have tempted me now these ten times, and have not hearkened to my voice;

Surely they shall not see the land which I sware unto their fathers, neither shall any of them that provoked me see it.

NUMBERS 14:22–23

See also Ex. 3:20; 7:3; 34:10; Mosiah 3:5; 4 Ne. 1:5.

As a result of the many miracles in our lives, we should be more humble and more grateful, more kind and more believing. When we are personal witnesses to these wonders which God performs, it should increase our respect and love for him; it should improve the way we behave. We will live better and love more if we will remember that.

(Howard W. Hunter, *The Teachings of Howard W. Hunter* [Salt Lake City: Bookcraft, 1997], 115.)

JULY 22
Seek God through Prayer

But if from thence thou shalt seek the Lord thy God, thou shalt find him, if thou seek him with all thy heart and with all thy soul.

DEUTERONOMY 4:29

See also 2 Chr. 15:4; Job 27:9; 2 Ne. 4:35; Moro. 7:48.

The channel by which we seek Him and find Him is personal and family prayer. The recognition of a power higher than man himself does not in any sense debase him; rather, it exalts him. Divine favor will attend those who humbly seek it.

(Thomas S. Monson, *Be Your Best Self* [Salt Lake City: Deseret Book, 1979], 97.)

JULY 23
Overcoming Fear

After these things the word of the Lord came unto Abram in a vision, saying, Fear not, Abram: I am thy shield, and thy exceeding great reward.

GENESIS 15:1

See also Ex. 20:20; Matt. 8:26; 2 Tim. 1:7; 1 Jn. 4:18.

Yes, love is the key to overcoming fear. In the Doctrine and Covenants we read, "Therefore, be ye strong from henceforth; fear not, for the kingdom is yours." This is a great promise. Fear is a stifling feeling, a roadblock. It comes not from God. Through power from God that is ours for the asking, we can overcome fear and have the courage to move forward. The spirit of love, the yellow ribbons, hugs, smiles, kindnesses, service, knowing that people are more important than possessions—these add flowers, sunshine, and joy as we travel along the road to our inheritance in the kingdom of God.

(Marvin J. Ashton, *Ye Are My Friends* [Salt Lake City: Deseret Book, 1972], 23–24.)

JULY 24
Gratitude

Now therefore, our God, we thank thee, and praise thy glorious name.

1 CHRONICLES 29:13
See also 2 Sam. 22:50; 1 Chr. 16:4, 7.

Let us then this day give, without stint, praise and gratitude to the pioneers for the heritage they passed to us. This we owe them for our material blessings not only, but for the pure blood flowing through our veins, for our strong bodies and sound minds, and for our knowledge of God's divine laws. Let us not be unmindful of the one and only way in which we *can* do them full honor. Let us seek testimonies the like of which they had, thus possessing ourselves of that vital moving faith which gave them and will give us purpose and direction in our living and wisdom and moral courage beyond our natural powers.

(Marion G. Romney, in F. Burton Howard, *Marion G. Romney: His Life and Faith* [Salt Lake City: Bookcraft, 1988], 252.)

JULY 25
Be a Good Neighbor

Lord, who shall abide in thy tabernacle? who shall dwell in thy holy hill? . . .

He that backbiteth not with his tongue, nor doeth evil to his neighbour, nor taketh up a reproach against his neighbour.

PSALM 15:1, 3

See also Lev. 19:13, 18; Matt. 19:19; Mosiah 23:15.

We can seek to be good neighbors. In most cases, those who are good neighbors will have good neighbors. Being a good neighbor means doing more than offering a thoughtful gesture from time to time on a holiday or crisis. It means striving continuously to build and maintain genuine friendship. . . . We can seek to provide selfless service because of the love we have for our fellowmen.

(Joseph B. Wirthlin, *Finding Peace in Our Lives* [Salt Lake City: Deseret Book,1995], 132.)

JULY 26
Temple Worthiness

And he set the porters at the gates of the house of the Lord, that none which was unclean in any thing should enter in.

2 Chronicles 23:19

See also Isa. 2:3; D&C 97:15; 109:19–20.

Those who come to these holy houses are arrayed in white as they participate therein. They come only on recommendation of their local ecclesiastical authorities, having been certified as to their worthiness. They are expected to come clean in thought, clean in body, and clean in dress to enter the temple of God. As they enter they are expected to leave the world behind them and concentrate on things divine.

This very exercise, if such it may be called, carries with it a reward of its own, for who in these times of stress would not welcome an occasional opportunity to shut out the world and enter into the Lord's house, there to ponder quietly the eternal things of God?

(Gordon B. Hinckley, *Be Thou an Example* [Salt Lake City: Deseret Book, 1981], 132.)

JULY 27

The Spirit of Temple Service

And they came, every one whose heart stirred him up, and every one whom his spirit made willing, and they brought the Lord's offering to the work of the tabernacle of the congregation, and for all his service, and for the holy garments.

EXODUS 35:21

See also Ex. 40:12–13; Mal. 4:5–6; 1 Cor. 15:29; D&C 2:2.

Yet there are immediate rewards for such vicarious service. Every time a person receives the temple endowment for another, he reviews the eternal journey of man, is reminded of the conditions of eternal progress and of his own covenants to obey God's law, is impressed anew with the necessity of making truth alive by use, and beholds again the glorious destiny of righteous man. His memory is refreshed, his conscience warned, his hopes lifted heavenward. Temple repetition is the mother of daily blessings. Wherever one turns, temple service profits those who perform it.

(John A. Widstoe, *Improvement Era* 39 [April 1936], 228.)

JULY 28
Covenant to Serve the Lord

Ye stand this day all of you before the Lord your
God . . .

That thou shouldest enter into covenant with
the Lord thy God, and into his oath, which the Lord
thy God maketh with thee this day.

DEUTERONOMY 29:10, 12

See also Ex. 19:5; 31:16; Jer. 50:5; Mosiah 18:13.

At baptism, we covenant to serve the Lord and
keep His commandments. When we partake of
the sacrament, we renew those covenants. We may
receive covenants of the priesthood and the crowning
blessings of the endowment, the doctrine, and the
covenants unique to the holy temple.

The new and everlasting covenant of the gospel
allows us to qualify for marriage in the temple and
be blessed to "come forth in the first resurrection"
and "inherit thrones, kingdoms, principalities, and
powers, dominions, . . . to [our] exaltation and glory
in all things."

(Russell M. Nelson, *Perfection Pending, and Other Favorite
Discourses* [Salt Lake City: Deseret Book, 1998], 191.)

JULY 29
Hearken to the Word of God

And it shall be, when he sitteth upon the throne of his kingdom, that he shall write him a copy of this law in a book out of that which is before the priests the Levites:

And it shall be with him, and he shall read therein all the days of his life: that he may learn to fear the Lord his God, to keep all the words of this law and these statutes, to do them.

DEUTERONOMY 17:18–19

See also Deut. 8:3; Josh. 8:34; 2 Ne. 32:3; Mosiah 1:5.

Scripture study as individuals and as a family is most fundamental to learning the gospel. Daily reading of the scriptures and discussing them together has long been suggested as a powerful tool against ignorance and the temptations of Satan. This practice will produce great happiness and will help family members love the Lord and his goodness. . . . Home is where we become experts and scholars in gospel righteousness.

(Spencer W. Kimball, *The Teachings of Spencer W. Kimball* [Salt Lake City: Bookcraft, 1982], 129.)

And Abraham planted a grove in Beersheba, and called there on the name of the Lord, the everlasting God.

GENESIS 21:33

See also 2 Kgs. 19:4; Mark 11:24–25; Alma 37:37; D&C 10:5.

I pray for strength; I pray for help; and I pray for the faith and the will to be obedient. I think that I need—and I feel that all of us need—discipline, if this great work is to roll forward as it is ordained to do.

(Russell M. Nelson, *The Power within Us* [Salt Lake City: Deseret Book, 1988], 143.)

JULY 31
Overcoming Pride

Pride goeth before destruction, and an haughty spirit before a fall.

Better it is to be of an humble spirit with the lowly, than to divide the spoil with the proud.

PROVERBS 16:18–19

See also Prov. 8:13; 13:10; 2 Ne. 28:15; Jacob 2:16.

Differences in knowledge, prominence, or position can also be sources of the pride of comparison. . . . No matter how prominent or praised, the preacher is no better than the hearer, the teacher is no better than the learner. To avoid pride, preachers and teachers and others in prominent positions must struggle not to esteem themselves above their hearers.

(Dallin H. Oaks, *Pure in Heart* [Salt Lake City: Bookcraft, 1988], 143–44.)

AUGUST

*I cried by reason of mine affliction
unto the Lord, and he heard me . . .*

—JONAH 2:2

AUGUST 1

Teach and Train Your Children

Train up a child in the way he should go: and when he is old, he will not depart from it.

PROVERBS 22:6

See also Deut. 4:10; Isa. 54:13; Mosiah 4:14–15.

Bring up your children in the love and fear of the Lord; . . . teach them to love you rather than to fear you, and let it be your constant care that the children that God has so kindly given you are taught in their early youth the importance of the oracles of God, and the beauty of the principles of our holy religion, . . . and never forsake the truth.

(Brigham Young, *Discourses of Brigham Young* [Salt Lake City: Deseret Book, 1954], 207.)

AUGUST 2
A Time and Season for All Things

To every thing there is a season, and a time to every purpose under the heaven.

ECCLESIASTES 3:1

See also Eccl. 3:2–8; Mark 1:15; Alma 34:30–34.

There can be a time and place for certain service. A mother with six young children in her household might not find those years to be the years when she can do as much community service as later on. . . . A student going to medical school can do his basic Church assignments and be an effective husband and father, but those years are probably not the years when he could contribute as much time as he desires to fund-raising for the local symphony.

Basically, if we are properly motivated and are proper managers of our time, there is a time and season for various good causes in our lives. The contributing emphasis, of course, must be upon keeping the commandments and being effective in our family life.

(Neal A. Maxwell, *Deposition of a Disciple* [Salt Lake City: Deseret Book, 1976], 69.)

AUGUST 3
Soft Answer

A soft answer turneth away wrath: but grievous words stir up anger.

PROVERBS 15:1

See also 1 Cor. 9:25; D&C 124:116.

Discipline with severity or with cruelty inevitably leads not to correction but to resentment and bitterness. It cures nothing; it only aggravates the problem. It is self-defeating. The Lord, in setting forth the spirit of governance in his church, has also set forth the spirit of governance in the home in these great words of revelation: "No power or influence can or ought to be maintained, . . . only by persuasion, by long-suffering, by gentleness and meekness, and by love unfeigned; . . . reproving betimes with sharpness, when moved upon by the Holy Ghost; and then showing forth afterwards an increase of love toward him whom thou hast reproved, lest he esteem thee to be his enemy; that he may know that thy faithfulness is stronger than the cords of death." . . . When little problems occur, as they inevitably will, restrain yourself.

(Gordon B. Hinckley, *Faith: The Essence of True Religion* [Salt Lake City: Deseret Book, 1989], 70–71.)

AUGUST 4
Be a Good Friend

A man that hath friends must shew himself friendly: and there is a friend that sticketh closer than a brother.

PROVERBS 18:24

See also Prov. 17:17; Eccl. 4:9–10.

Acts of a friend should result in self-improvement, better attitudes, self-reliance, comfort, consolation, self-respect, and better welfare. . . . It takes courage to be a real friend. Some of us endanger the valued classification of friend because of our unwillingness to be one under all circumstances. Fear can deprive us of friendship. Some of us identify our closest friends as those with the courage to remain and share themselves with us under all circumstances. A friend is a person who will suggest and render the best for us regardless of the immediate consequences.

(Marvin J. Ashton, "What Is a Friend?" *Ensign,* Jan. 1973, 41.)

AUGUST 5
Positive Attitude

A merry heart maketh a cheerful countenance: but by sorrow of the heart the spirit is broken.

PROVERBS 15:13

See also Ps. 100:1–5; 2 Cor. 9:7; D&C 19:39; 123:17.

The Savior reminds us, "All things are possible to him that believeth," and "All things shall work together for your good." The attitude with which we submit to "all things" is important. Maintaining a positive attitude and being cheerful are helpful. A belief that "all these things shall give thee experience, and shall be for thy good" is like a spiritual stabilizer.

(James E. Faust, *Reach Up for the Light* [Salt Lake City: Deseret Book, 1990], 83.)

AUGUST 6
Knowledge and Wisdom

Give instruction to a wise man, and he will be yet wiser: teach a just man, and he will increase in learning.

The fear of the Lord is the beginning of wisdom: and the knowledge of the holy is understanding.

PROVERBS 9:9-10

See also Prov. 4:7; 8:11; 9:10; 2 Ne. 28:30; Alma 37:35.

We are told that a man cannot be saved in ignorance. Therefore we list knowledge as the second essential ingredient of a successful life. We underline and emphasize the importance of continuing education, gaining knowledge, and the power that comes with knowledge.

But knowledge alone, without wisdom to use it properly, may be dangerous. We therefore list wisdom as the third essential. A well-educated man may be a very dangerous man if he lacks wisdom and character.

(Hugh B. Brown, *The Abundant Life* [Salt Lake City: Bookcraft, 1965], 230.)

AUGUST 7
Life Is a Test

And Moses said unto the people, Fear not: for God is come to prove you, and that his fear may be before your faces, that ye sin not.

EXODUS 20:20

See also Gen. 3:22; Job 1:12; 1 Cor. 10:13; Alma 42:4.

First Questioner: You stress the importance of recognizing that life is a test and a proving place. Does accepting that doctrine make the test easier?

The Disciple: Knowing that one is in the midst of a testing time does not make the test any less real. The disciple is not able to wink slyly, as if he could cope with one hand tied behind him. His teeth rattle, too. It's "all out" for everybody, and then we scarcely make it.

The temptations of Jesus were terrifyingly real even though he did not yield. The difference is that those who are (or who will become) Saints reach breaking points without breaking. Often this is the very kind of humble report you hear at fast and testimony meetings—about the passing of one of those mortal milestones.

(Neal A. Maxwell, *Deposition of a Disciple* [Salt Lake City: Deseret Book, 1976], 52.)

AUGUST 8
Dealing with Adversity

In their affliction they will seek me early.

HOSEA 5:15

See also 2 Chr. 15:4; 2 Ne. 2:11–13; D&C 121:7–8.

Adversity touches many, many lives. What makes the difference is how we accept it. It's important to know it's all within the purposes of the Lord, whatever they are for us. If we can submit ourselves to that, we can go forward in faith and understanding.

(Howard W. Hunter, *The Teachings of Howard W. Hunter* [Salt Lake City: Bookcraft, 1997], 84.)

AUGUST 9
Strength in the Lord

Behold, God is mighty, and despiseth not any: he is mighty in strength and wisdom.

JOB 36:5

See also Ps. 118:14; Alma 26:10–12; Ether 12:26–27.

Christ walked the path every mortal is called to walk so that he would know how to succor and strengthen us in our most difficult times. He knows the deepest and most personal burdens we carry. He knows the most public and poignant pains we bear. He descended below all such grief in order that he might lift us above it. There is no anguish or sorrow or sadness in life that he has not suffered in our behalf and borne away upon his own valiant and compassionate shoulders. In so doing he "giveth power to the faint; and to them that have no might he increaseth strength. . . . [Thus] they that wait upon the Lord shall renew their strength; they shall mount up with wings as eagles; they shall run, and not be weary; and they shall walk, and not faint."

(Jeffrey R. Holland, *Christ and the New Covenant: The Messianic Message of the Book of Mormon* [Salt Lake City: Deseret Book, 1997], 223–24.)

AUGUST 10
Power in Righteousness

Sow to yourselves in righteousness, reap in mercy; break up your fallow ground: for it is time to seek the Lord, till he come and rain righteousness upon you.

HOSEA 10:12

See also 1 Ne. 14:14; D&C 58:26–28; 121:36.

The nature of this service is spelled out in detail in the revelations and by the living prophets. The Lord has laid the burden of it upon his priesthood. It can be done properly only by men who are magnifying their callings in the priesthood; who know the gospel; who conform their lives to its standards; and who enthusiastically give dedicated service in the spirit of the divine proclamation that "men should be anxiously engaged in a good cause, and do many things of their own free will, and bring to pass much righteousness: For the power is in them."

(Marion G. Romney, *Learning for the Eternities* [Salt Lake City: Deseret Book, 1977], 92.)

AUGUST 11
Endure to the End

God forbid that I should justify you: till I die I will not remove mine integrity from me.

Job 27:5

See also Ruth 1:18; Job 2:3; Matthew 24:13; 1 Ne. 13:37.

The culminating requirement repeatedly stated in the scriptures is that we must endure to the end: "And as many as . . . endure to the end, the same shall be saved." "And . . . if thou endure it well, God shall exalt thee on high; thou shalt triumph over all thy foes."

(Neal A. Maxwell, *If Thou Endure It Well* [Salt Lake City: Bookcraft, 1996], 39.)

AUGUST 12
Blessings to the Faithful

Blessed are all they that put their trust in him.

PSALM 2:12

See also Ps. 119:1–2; 1 Cor. 2:9; James 1:12; 1 Ne. 17:2.

If we desire further blessings of the Lord, we should not expect to receive them only upon further compliance with His laws. Obedience to one requirement does not entitle us to all blessings; and yet we should seek to gain all the blessings promised to the faithful. The gifts of our Heavenly Father ought to be highly prized by everyone, and they should be diligently sought after. Just how they are to be obtained is made plain by the Prophet in the words already quoted—"When we obtain any blessing from God, it is by obedience to that law upon which it is predicated."

(George Q. Cannon, *Gospel Truth: Discourses and Writings of President George Q. Cannon* [Salt Lake City: Deseret Book, 1987], C.)

AUGUST 13
Leave Judgment to the Lord

For God shall bring every work into judgment, with every secret thing, whether it be good, or whether it be evil.

ECCLESIASTES 12:14

See also Ex. 12:12; 1 Sam. 2:10; Matt. 7:2; 3 Ne. 14:1–2.

Meaningful progress can be made only when all of us can cast the motes out of our own eyes, leave judgment to our Father in heaven, and lose ourselves in righteous living.

(Marvin J. Ashton, *Be of Good Cheer* [Salt Lake City: Deseret Book, 1987], 10.)

AUGUST 14
We Are Called to Proclaim the Gospel

The Spirit of the Lord God is upon me; because the Lord hath anointed me to preach good tidings unto the meek; he hath sent me to bind up the broken-hearted, to proclaim liberty to the captives, and the opening of the prison to them that are bound.

ISAIAH 61:1

See also 1 Chr.16:24; 2 Chr. 24:19; Jonah 3:2; Mark 16:15.

We live in the most exciting era in the history of mankind. The potential for declaring the gospel to the peoples of the world has never been greater. . . . The Book of Mormon has been translated into many languages, making available this great doctrinal base of scripture to so many more of our Heavenly Father's children. It is opening the way for their understanding of the blessings attendant to living the Lord's law. . . . How exciting it is to live in this great day and be called to labor and bear testimony of the great work in which we are now engaged!

(L. Tom Perry, "Proclaim My Gospel from Land to Land," *Ensign,* May 1989, 13.)

AUGUST 15
Declare Repentance

Arise, go to Nineveh, that great city, and cry against it; for their wickedness is come up before me.

JONAH 1:2

See also Ezra 10:11; Neh. 9:2; Matt. 4:17; Mosiah 18:20.

Once settled in "holy places," the task for the disciple is to "stand . . . and . . . not be moved." Those who waver in their steadfastness for fear they are missing out will miss out. Those who fret lest the seeming mundaneness of their mortal passage implies that they thereby are shortchanged would do well to recall what those were told who inquired of the Lord as to what they could do of "most worth" to help His work along. They were told, quite simply, to get their lives in order and to declare repentance unto this generation. No mention was made of improving Congress or a nation's monetary policy, important as these may be for the moment.

(Neal A. Maxwell, *We Will Prove Them Herewith* [Salt Lake City: Deseret Book, 1982], 51–52.)

AUGUST 16
Fear Not to Preach the Gospel

And Moses answered and said, But, behold, they
will not believe me, nor hearken unto my voice: for
they will say, The Lord hath not appeared unto thee.

EXODUS 4:1

See also Ezek. 3:27; D&C 24:12; 33:8–10; 60:2–3.

We made a commitment at baptism that we
would stand as witnesses of God at all times, and in
all places, and in all things. It is our duty. . . . We
must understand that if we just have the courage,
and overcome fear and doubt, then we can open our
mouths, and they will be filled.

(Ed J. Pinegar, *The Ultimate Missionary Companion*
[American Fork, UT: Covenant Communications, 2001], 82.)

AUGUST 17
Pure Testimony

And all flesh shall know that I the Lord am thy Saviour and thy Redeemer, the mighty One of Jacob.

ISAIAH 49:26

See also Ex. 31:18; Ps. 132:12; 1 Jn. 4:15; Mosiah 18:9.

That is our message to the world. . . . Our mission becomes all the more urgent in calling men to repentance and to a belief in the redemption brought to pass through the atonement of the Son of God, whose blood was shed for the sins of the world. . . .

It is our message and our mission to the world to preach this truth, and to establish faith in the hearts of the people, and endeavor to get them to believe in Jesus Christ as their Redeemer and as the Son of God.

(Joseph Fielding Smith, *Doctrines of Salvation* [Salt Lake City: Bookcraft, 1954–1956], 1:308–09.)

AUGUST 18
Teach the Word of God by the Spirit

And thou shalt teach them diligently unto thy children, and shalt talk of them when thou sittest in thine house, and when thou walkest by the way, and when thou liest down, and when thou risest up.

DEUTERONOMY 6:7

See also 2 Sam. 23:2; Neh. 9:20; Alma 29:13; 31:5.

We are of Israel, and the covenants made with our fathers are now being fulfilled. We are called to preach the everlasting word in all the world that our scattered brethren of the house of Jacob may all hear the message, be gathered into the fold of their Ancient Shepherd, and there find refreshment with all his sheep.

(Bruce R. McConkie, *The Millennial Messiah: The Second Coming of the Son of Man* [Salt Lake City: Deseret Book, 1982], 145.)

AUGUST 19
Be a Light

I the Lord have called thee in righteousness, and will hold thine hand, and will keep thee, and give thee for a covenant of the people, for a light of the Gentiles;

To open the blind eyes, to bring out the prisoners from the prison, and them that sit in darkness out of the prison house.

ISAIAH 42:6–7

See also Isa. 60:3; D&C 49:11–14; 88:81; 106:2; 124:106.

It is generally understood that every member of the Church should be a missionary. He is probably not authorized to go from house to house, but he is authorized by virtue of his membership to set a proper example as a good neighbor. Neighbors are watching him. He is a "light," and it is his duty not to have that "light" hidden under a bushel; but it should be set upon a hill that all men may be guided thereby.

(David O. McKay, *Man May Know for Himself: Teachings of President David O. McKay* [Salt Lake City: Deseret Book, 1967], 129.)

AUGUST 20
Pruning of the Vineyard

For the vineyard of the Lord of hosts is the house of Israel, and the men of Judah his pleasant plant: and he looked for judgment, but behold oppression; for righteousness, but behold a cry. . . .

And he will lift up an ensign to the nations from far, and will hiss unto them from the end of the earth: and, behold, they shall come with speed swiftly.

Isaiah 5:7, 26

See also Jacob 5:71; D&C 24:19; 138:56.

Beautiful, luscious fruit does not grow unless the roots of the parent tree have been planted in rich, fertile soil and unless due care is given to proper pruning, cultivation, and irrigation. So likewise the luscious fruits of virtue and chastity, honesty, temperance, integrity, and fidelity are not to be found growing in that individual whose life is not founded on a firm testimony of the truths of the gospel and of the life and the mission of the Lord Jesus Christ. To be truly righteous there is required a daily pruning of the evil growth of our characters by daily repentance from sin.

(Harold B. Lee, "'Successful' Sinners," *Ensign,* July 1971, 2.)

AUGUST 21
The Lord Is Merciful

The Lord is merciful and gracious, slow to anger, and plenteous in mercy.

PSALM 103:8

See also Ex. 34:6; Alma 12:33; D&C 110:7.

Early in my ministry . . . I took to President Hugh B. Brown the experience of a fine person who could not serve in a ward position because he could not show mercy to himself. He could forgive others but not himself; mercy was seemingly beyond his grasp. President Brown suggested that I visit with that individual and counsel him along these lines: "I, the Lord, will forgive whom I will forgive, but of you it is required to forgive all men. . . . Though your sins be as scarlet, they shall be as white as snow; though they be red like crimson, they shall be as wool." "Behold, he who has repented of his sins, the same is forgiven, and I, the Lord, remember them no more."

With a pensive expression on his face, President Brown added: "Tell that man that he should not persist in remembering that which the Lord has said He is willing to forget."

(Thomas S. Monson, "Mercy—The Divine Gift," *Ensign*, May 1995, 59–60.)

AUGUST 22
The Lord Loves Us

I will heal their backsliding, I will love them freely: for mine anger is turned away from him.

HOSEA 14:4

See also Hosea 11:1–4; Jacob 3:2.

Just as the love of God for us is unconditional, one day ours for Him must be likewise. This is what the first commandment is all about. But even then, the adoration and awe we have developed for God will take humble notice of the eternal fact, stressed by John, that God loved us first. As we come closer to Him, we not only "stand all amazed"—we even kneel all amazed!

(Neal A. Maxwell, *Notwithstanding My Weakness* [Salt Lake City: Deseret Book, 1981], 33.)

AUGUST 23
Be True to Our Covenants

And thou shalt observe to keep all my covenants wherein I covenanted with thy fathers; and thou shalt keep the commandments which I have given thee with mine own mouth, and I will be a God unto thee and thy seed after thee.

JST, Genesis 17:12

See also Ex. 39:32; Deut. 6:17; 1 Ne. 17:40; 2 Ne. 11:5.

It is for each of us to be loyal and true, to keep our covenants. Keep your spiritual premiums paid up. Do not let your spiritual policy lapse. Do not cause it to be cancelled in some moment of rebellion. Extend your policy by adding endorsements as you qualify for the higher ordinances of the gospel. Make a list of them, keep them in mind, work to qualify for each of them. And pray earnestly for help to do so.

I was always impressed when President Joseph Fielding Smith was asked to pray. Invariably, he would make reference to the principles and ordinances of the gospel and always would include the expression, "May we remain faithful to our covenants and obligations."

(Boyd K. Packer, *The Holy Temple* [Salt Lake City: Bookcraft, 1980], 168.)

AUGUST 24

We Are Commanded to Repent

❦

But if the wicked will turn from all his sins that he hath committed, and keep all my statutes, and do that which is lawful and right, he shall surely live, he shall not die.

All his transgressions that he hath committed, they shall not be mentioned unto him: in his righteousness that he hath done he shall live.

EZEKIEL 18:21–22

See also Ps. 51:10; Prov. 28:13; Alma 9:12; 3 Ne. 27:20.

The doctrine of repentance is an essential part of the Gospel. It occupies the second place in the Articles of Faith of the Church: (1) Faith; (2) Repentance; (3) Baptism: (4) Laying on of hands for the reception of the Holy Ghost. But repentance is not only a doctrine. It is the main manifestation of the new life of those who have been "born again" and thereby became citizens of the kingdom of God. All are commanded to repent, and genuine repentance brings forgiveness.

(George Reynolds and Janne M. Sjodahl, *Commentary on the Book of Mormon* [Salt Lake City: Deseret Book, 1955–1961], 1:302.)

AUGUST 25
The Commandments Bless Our Lives

Keep the commandments of the Lord, and his statutes, which I command thee this day for thy good.

DEUTERONOMY 10:13

See also Ezra 9:14; JST, Matt. 16:27; Jarom 1:9; Mosiah 2:22.

When we break the commandments, we close ourselves to God's influence and open ourselves to Satan's influence.

(Joseph B. Wirthlin, *Finding Peace in Our Lives* [Salt Lake City: Deseret Book, 1995], 183.)

AUGUST 26
Breaking the Commandments Brings Sorrow

If they break my statutes, and keep not my commandments;

Then will I visit their transgression with the rod, and their iniquity with stripes.

PSALM 89:31–32

See also Deut. 30:16; 1 Ne. 17:13–15; Mosiah 2:41.

During these troublous times when so many are in distress, seeking happiness and not finding it, I think the finest recipe that I could give to obtain happiness would be: Keep the commandments of the Lord. That is easy to remember, and if we will do that we may be sure of success.

All down through the ages the Lord has inspired his choice servants and they have taught the people the gospel, they have pointed out the way of true happiness.

(George Albert Smith, *The Teachings of George Albert Smith* [Salt Lake City: Bookcraft, 1996], 95.)

AUGUST 27
Forgiveness Is Divine

I acknowledged my sin unto thee, and mine iniquity have I not hid. I said, I will confess my transgressions unto the Lord; and thou forgavest the iniquity of my sin.

Psalm 32:5

See also Ex. 34:7, 9; Num. 15:25; Mosiah 26:30; D&C 1:32.

If we have been wronged or injured, forgiveness means to blot it completely from our minds. To forgive and forget is an ageless counsel. "To be wronged or robbed," said the Chinese philosopher Confucius, "is nothing unless you continue to remember it."

The injuries inflicted by neighbors, by relatives, or by spouses are generally of a minor nature, at least at first. We must forgive them. Since the Lord is so merciful, must not we be? "Blessed are the merciful, for they shall obtain mercy" is another version of the golden rule. "All manner of sin and blasphemy shall be forgiven unto men," said the Lord, "but the blasphemy against the Holy Ghost shall not be forgiven unto men." If the Lord is so gracious and kind, we must be also.

(Spencer W. Kimball, *The Miracle of Forgiveness* [Salt Lake City: Bookcraft, 1969], 299.)

AUGUST 28
Study the Scriptures

Every word of God is pure: he is a shield unto them that put their trust in him.

PROVERBS 30:5

See also 1 Sam. 9:27; Luke 4:4; 2 Ne. 32:3; Mormon 8:16.

We should read the Bible, the Book of Mormon, the Doctrine and Covenants, and the Pearl of Great Price; not only read it in our homes, but explain it to our children, that they may understand the hand dealings of God with the peoples of the earth. Let us see if we cannot do more of this in the future than we have done in the past. Let each one in this congregation today ask himself: "Have I done my duty in my home in reading and in teaching the gospel, as it has been revealed through the prophets of the Lord?" If we have not let us repent of our neglect and draw our families around us and teach them the truth.

(George Albert Smith, *The Teachings of George Albert Smith* [Salt Lake City: Bookcraft, 1996], 127–28.)

AUGUST 29
Prophets Speak for the Lord

And the Lord said unto Enoch: Go forth and do as I have commanded thee, and no man shall pierce thee. Open thy mouth, and it shall be filled, and I will give thee utterance, for all flesh is in my hands, and I will do as seemeth me good.

MOSES 6:32

See also Ex. 4:12, 16; 2 Sam. 23:2; Hel. 13:4–5.

What is a prophet? How may we test a man who claims to be a prophet? Is there some measuring rod by which we may determine the validity of his claim? I define a prophet as one who speaks for God; one who predicts the things to come; one to whom God has spoken. . . . All the prophets of whom we have record—and there were, according to Jewish reckoning, forty-eight prophets between Adam and Malachi—every one of them began his ministry with the solemn declaration, "God has spoken to me." And each of them followed that declaration again and again with the unequivocal statement, "Thus saith the Lord." . . . These prophets merely said, "Thus saith the Lord." They were his witnesses and messengers.

(Hugh B. Brown, *Continuing the Quest* [Salt Lake City: Deseret Book, 1961], 141.)

AUGUST 30
Hearken to the Prophet and Live

But they hearkened not, nor inclined their ear to turn from their wickedness, to burn no incense unto other gods.

Wherefore my fury and mine anger was poured forth, and was kindled in the cities of Judah and in the streets of Jerusalem; and they are wasted and desolate, as at this day.

JEREMIAH 44:5–6

See also 2 Kgs. 17:14; 2 Chr. 24:21, 23; 36:16; 1 Ne. 3:17.

Though often humble by the world's measure. . . . It would be wisdom on all occasions and with respect to all subjects in any field of human activity, to hearken to the prophet's voice. There is safety and ultimate happiness in following the counsel that may be received from the prophet.

(John A. Widtsoe, *Evidences and Reconciliations* [Salt Lake City: Improvement Era], 237.)

AUGUST 31

Turn to the Lord

Therefore also now, saith the Lord, turn ye even to me with all your heart, and with fasting, and with weeping, and with mourning:

And rend your heart, and not your garments, and turn unto the Lord your God: for he is gracious and merciful, slow to anger, and of great kindness, and repenteth him of the evil.

JOEL 2:12–13

See also Deut. 4:30; Hosea 14:2; Mosiah 7:33; 11:21.

The gospel of Jesus Christ is the *only true and valid basis* for our lives. If we enter it into our system—into "all [our] heart, might, mind and strength"—we will know how to choose the right and to whom to listen. . . . Jesus Christ, the Son of God, made the miracle of forgiveness and redemption possible. This is truly the Church of Jesus Christ; it proclaims a gospel of joy, hope, courage, truth, love, and miracles.

(Dieter F. Uchtdorf, "The Only True and Valid Basis," *Ensign,* Nov. 1994, 41.)

EPTEMBER

*I have enough, my brother; keep that
thou hast unto thyself.*

—GENESIS 33:9

SEPTEMBER 1
The Lord Is Our Hope

But the Lord will be the hope of his people, and the strength of the children of Israel.

JOEL 3:16

See also 1 Jn. 3:2–3; Ether 12:32; Moro. 8:26.

In and through and by and because of him we and all men have a hope of peace in this life and eternal glory in the world to come. He is our Hope. Without him we would have no hope of immortality, no hope of eternal life, no hope of the continuation of the family unit, no hope of eternal progress, no hope of exaltation, no hope of any good thing. All the hopes of all the righteous of all the ages center in him. . . .

"We are saved by hope," and the "Lord Jesus Christ . . . is our hope," said Paul. The lives of the righteous are spent "looking for that blessed hope," he also said, which hope is for "the glorious appearing of the great God and our Saviour Jesus Christ."

(Bruce R. McConkie, *The Promised Messiah: The First Coming of Christ* [Salt Lake City: Deseret Book, 1978], 183–84.)

SEPTEMBER 2
The Spirit Shall Be Poured Out

And it shall come to pass afterward, that I will pour out my spirit upon all flesh; and your sons and your daughters shall prophesy, your old men shall dream dreams, your young men shall see visions:

And also upon the servants and upon the handmaids in those days will I pour out my spirit.

JOEL 2:28–29

See also Neh. 9:20; Ezek. 11:5; Alma 19:36; 3 Ne. 7:21.

Having described the Restoration as his "Strange act," and "my strange work," the Lord indicated that it would go against the grain of much of society. Yet restitution of the unfamiliar, the uncommon, the unusual, and the unique would actually aid mortals by providing fresh, divine standards and help them in discerning between righteousness and wickedness, as God "poured out [His] Spirit upon all flesh."

(Neal A. Maxwell, *A Wonderful Flood of Light* [Salt Lake City: Bookcraft, 1990], 9.)

SEPTEMBER 3
Beware of Ease

Woe to them that are at ease in Zion.

AMOS 6:1

See also Isa. 32:9, 11; 2 Ne. 28:24; Hel. 12:2.

We must not forget the source of all our blessings—our prosperity, our wealth, our comforts, our freedom. We must not forget that it is by God's gracious hand that these blessings are preserved, and not by our own superior wisdom. May we keep alive our faith in God by worshiping Him and keeping His commandments.

(Ezra Taft Benson, *This Nation Shall Endure* [Salt Lake City: Deseret Book, 1977], 87.)

SEPTEMBER 4
The Last Days

Their land also is full of idols; they worship the work of their own hands, that which their own fingers have made.

ISAIAH 2:8

See also Isa. 1:3–5, 11–15; 2:11–12; 3:9,14–24; 5:8, 20, 21.

Surely we see these indications prevalent in our own land and in foreign lands. Men have become carnal. They have become enemies to God. They are seeking for their own advancement and not for the advancement of the kingdom of God. Let me call your attention to this fact which you, of course, all know, that we are living in the last days, the days of trouble, days of wickedness.

(Joseph Fielding Smith, *Doctrines of Salvation* [Salt Lake City: Bookcraft, 1954–1956], 3:280.)

SEPTEMBER 5
Do Good and Be Blessed

If thou doest well, shalt thou not be accepted? and if thou doest not well, sin lieth at the door.

GENESIS 4:7

See also Isa. 1:18; Eph. 6:11–17; Alma 13:28–29; 3 Ne. 18:18.

Put on the full armor of God. Attend to your personal and family prayers and family devotions; keep holy the Sabbath; live strictly the Word of Wisdom; attend to all family duties; and above all, keep your life clean and free from all unholy and impure thoughts and actions. Avoid all associations that degrade and lower the high, righteous standards set up for us. Then your life will sail smoothly, and peace and joy will surround you.

(Spencer W. Kimball, *President Kimball Speaks Out* [Salt Lake City: Deseret Book, 1981], 17.)

SEPTEMBER 6
Stand in Holy Places

For thou art an holy people unto the Lord thy God, and the Lord hath chosen thee to be a peculiar people unto himself, above all the nations that are upon the earth.

DEUTERONOMY 14:2

See also Ex. 19:6; Lev. 19:2; Num. 16:5; Isaiah 4:5–6.

God grant that it may be so for all those whose minds are distressed and who are worried and frightened during these disturbing times. "My disciples shall stand in holy places, and . . . not be moved." ". . . watch, therefore, for you know not at what hour your Lord doth come." The Lord's promises are sure, and His word will not fail.

(Harold B. Lee, *Stand Ye in Holy Places* [Salt Lake City: Deseret Book, 1974], 24–25.)

SEPTEMBER 7
Gathering Israel

That then the Lord thy God will turn thy captivity, and have compassion upon thee, and will return and gather thee from all the nations, whither the Lord thy God hath scattered thee.

DEUTERONOMY 30:3

See also Isa. 5:26–29; 10:22; 27:12; Jer. 23:3; 29:14.

It is a matter of historical record that God said he would scatter Israel. It is a matter of historical record that he said he would gather Israel from the four corners of the earth. And this congregation today is a witness to the world that it is a matter of historical fact that through the Church of Jesus Christ of Latter-day Saints, God is gathering Israel.

(Matthew Cowley, *Matthew Cowley Speaks* [Salt Lake City: Deseret Book, 1954], 25.)

SEPTEMBER 8
Honor Your Callings

Also I heard the voice of the Lord, saying, Whom shall I send, and who will go for us? Then said I, Here am I; send me.

ISAIAH 6:8

See also Num. 27:23; Jer. 1:7; 1 Ne. 2:3; 3:7; A of F 1:5.

For what is the priesthood conferred upon you? Is it to follow the "devices and desires of your own hearts," as I used to hear them say in the Church of England when I was a boy? Is it to do that? I think not. Or were we enlisted to God, for time and eternity? I think we were; and we want to wake up to the responsibilities which devolve upon us, and honor our calling and magnify our priesthood.

(John Taylor, *The Gospel Kingdom: Selections from the Writings and Discourses of John Taylor* [Salt Lake City: Improvement Era, 1941], 199.)

SEPTEMBER 9
Discern between Good and Evil

Woe unto them that call evil good, and good evil; that put darkness for light, and light for darkness; that put bitter for sweet, and sweet for bitter!

ISAIAH 5:20

See also Gen. 3:22; Ps. 73:24; 2 Ne. 32:5; Moro. 7:15–17.

There is a defense mechanism to discern between good and evil. It is called conscience. It is our spirit's natural response to the pain of sin, just like pain in our flesh is our body's natural response to a wound—even a small sliver. Conscience strengthens through use. Paul told the Hebrews, "But strong meat belongeth to them that are of full age, even those who by reason of use have their senses exercised to discern both good and evil." Those who have not exercised their conscience have "their conscience seared with a hot iron." A sensitive conscience is a sign of a healthy spirit.

(James E. Faust, *Finding Light in a Dark World* [Salt Lake City: Deseret Book, 1995], 18–19.)

SEPTEMBER 10
The Lord's Succor

I will mention the lovingkindnesses of the Lord, and the praises of the Lord, according to all that the Lord hath bestowed on us, and the great goodness toward the house of Israel, which he hath bestowed on them according to his mercies, and according to the multitude of his lovingkindnesses.

For he said, Surely they are my people, children that will not lie: so he was their Saviour.

Isaiah 63:7–8

See also Deut. 7:8; Heb. 10:10; Alma 7:11–12; D&C 62:1.

The Lord has also clearly promised to succor us in the midst of our temptations. . . . Such divine, close-in support as is promised in the scriptures means that God's grace will be sufficient for us if we are humble.

However, we must turn ourselves over to the Lord, so that we can be succored by Him and so that our weaknesses can even become strengths.

(Neal A. Maxwell, *Notwithstanding My Weakness* [Salt Lake City: Deseret Book, 1981], 14.)

SEPTEMBER 11

The Firstborn and Only Begotten in the Flesh

Also I will make him my firstborn, higher than the kings of the earth.

PSALM 89:27

See also Ps. 2:7; Isa. 7:14; 9:6; John 1:14; Moses 4:2.

Knowing that Jesus Christ is the Firstborn Son of God in the spirit and the Only Begotten Son in the flesh gives a far more noble and majestic view of him than if he were just a great teacher or philosopher. He is our Lord, the Redeemer of all mankind, our Mediator with the Father. Because of his love for us, he has atoned for the sins of the world and has provided a way for the faithful to return to the presence of our Heavenly Father.

(Joseph B. Wirthlin, *Finding Peace in Our Lives* [Salt Lake City: Deseret Book, 1995], 40–41.)

SEPTEMBER 12

The Savior Cares for Those in Spirit Prison

And they shall be gathered together, as prisoners are gathered in the pit, and shall be shut up in the prison, and after many days shall they be visited.

Isaiah 24:22

See also Isa. 42:5–7; 49:9–10; D&C 88:99; 138:29–37, 57.

Their spirits were committed to a prison which the Lord had prepared for them, and there they remained in torment, being punished for their great wickedness, until the crucifixion of the Savior. After His Spirit left His body, He went and opened the prison doors to them and declared to them the Gospel of salvation. They then had the opportunity of repenting.

(George Q. Cannon, *Gospel Truth: Discourses and Writings of President George Q. Cannon* [Salt Lake City: Deseret Book, 1987], 358.)

SEPTEMBER 13
The Savior Is Our Refuge

For thou hast been a strength to the poor, a strength to the needy in his distress, a refuge from the storm, a shadow from the heat, when the blast of the terrible ones is as a storm against the wall.

ISAIAH 25:4

See also 2 Sam. 22:3; Isa. 32:2; 2 Ne. 14:6; D&C 115:6.

Reach out to Him. He does answer prayers. He does bring peace. He does give hope. In the words of the Psalmist: "He is my refuge and my fortress: . . . in him will I trust." Study carefully the life of the Savior. He is our great exemplar.

Make the scriptures your constant companion. Read daily from the Book of Mormon and receive of its strength and spiritual power.

Realize your personal self-worth. Never demean yourself. Realize the strength of your inner self and that, with God's help, you "can do all things through Christ which strengtheneth [you]."

(Ezra Taft Benson, "To the Single Adult Sisters of the Church," *Ensign,* Nov. 1988, 97.)

SEPTEMBER 14

The Savior Brings Forth the Resurrection

Thy dead men shall live, together with my dead body shall they arise. Awake and sing, ye that dwell in dust: for thy dew is as the dew of herbs, and the earth shall cast out the dead.

ISAIAH 26:19

See also 1 Sam. 2:6; 2 Ne. 2:6–9; 9:4–9; D&C 133:52–56.

Joseph Smith's vision of man's immortal nature reached from an existence before birth to the eternities beyond the grave. He taught that salvation is universal in that all men will become the beneficiaries of the resurrection through the atonement wrought by the Savior. But beyond this gift is the requirement of obedience to the principles of the gospel and the promise of consequent happiness in this life and exaltation in the life to come.

(Gordon B. Hinckley, *Be Thou an Example* [Salt Lake City: Deseret Book, 1981], 120.)

SEPTEMBER 15
The Savior Is Our Foundation and King

Therefore thus saith the Lord God, Behold, I lay in Zion for a foundation a stone, a tried stone, a precious corner stone, a sure foundation: he that believeth shall not make haste.

ISAIAH 28:16

See also Zech. 14:9; Eph. 2:19–21; 1 Peter 2:6–8; Hel. 5:12.

As a constant reminder and guide for their actions, these brothers had in their hearts the words of their father, Helaman, who, in the spirit of the "man of Christ" declaration, had reminded them that "there is no other means whereby man can be saved, only through the atoning blood of Jesus Christ, who shall come; yea remember that he cometh to redeem the world. . . .

"Remember that it is upon the rock of our Redeemer, who is Christ, the Son of God, that ye must build your foundation . . . because of the rock upon which ye are built, which is a sure foundation, a foundation whereon if men build they cannot fall."

(Jeffrey R. Holland, *Christ and the New Covenant: The Messianic Message of the Book of Mormon* [Salt Lake City: Deseret Book, 1997], 129.)

And thou shalt be brought down, and shalt speak out of the ground, and thy speech shall be low out of the dust, and thy voice shall be, as of one that hath a familiar spirit, out of the ground, and thy speech shall whisper out of the dust.

ISAIAH 29:4

See also Gen. 49:22; Isa. 29:9–14,18,24; Ezek. 37:19.

With the restoration of the fulness of the gospel came the Book of Mormon, another testament of Jesus Christ. Other revelations were given and continue to be given as a result of which verses that seemed to oppose one another have harmony.

(Boyd K. Packer, *Let Not Your Heart Be Troubled* [Salt Lake City: Bookcraft, 1991], 292.)

SEPTEMBER 17
The Savior Directs Our Paths

And though the Lord give you the bread of adversity, and the water of affliction, yet shall not thy teachers be removed into a corner any more, but thine eyes shall see thy teachers:

And thine ears shall hear a word behind thee, saying, This is the way, walk ye in it, when ye turn to the right hand, and when ye turn to the left.

ISAIAH 30:20–21

See also Prov. 3:6; 1 Ne. 4:6; Alma 37:37; 48:15; D&C 112:10.

Certainly spiritual understanding and testimony are available to all who earnestly seek them. Elder Bruce R. McConkie has said: "And because God is no respecter of persons, everyone in the Church who will get on his knees and ask the Lord for guidance and direction will receive identically that same knowledge, that same assurance, and that same understanding."

(James E. Faust, *To Reach Even unto You* [Salt Lake City: Deseret Book, 1980], 12–13.)

SEPTEMBER 18
Our Lord Is the Only Savior

I, even I, am the Lord; and beside me there is no saviour.

ISAIAH 43:11

See also Ps. 27:1; Isa. 43:3, 25; 1 Jn. 2:1–2; 1 Ne. 13:40.

Since Christ is the Savior, since all things pertaining to life and salvation center in him, since he is God—it follows that all men must turn to him and his gospel for salvation, and that in his own due time he shall receive the worship and adoration of all men. Indeed, to all men, by the mouth of Isaiah, Israel's Jehovah said: "Look unto me, and be ye saved, all the ends of the earth: for I am God, and there is none else. I have sworn by myself, the word is gone out of my mouth in righteousness, and shall not return, That unto me every knee shall bow, every tongue shall swear."

(Bruce R. McConkie, *Doctrinal New Testament Commentary* [Salt Lake City: Bookcraft, 1965–1973], 2:533.)

SEPTEMBER 19

Jehovah—God of the Old Testament

Thus saith the Lord the King of Israel, and his redeemer the Lord of hosts; I am the first, and I am the last; and beside me there is no God.

Isaiah 44:6

See also Ex. 3:6; John 8:58; 1 Ne. 19:10; 2 Ne. 6:17.

The true significance therefore of the divine instruction and revelation which Moses received upon Mount Sinai, came from God the Eternal Father, through his first-born spirit Son of the pre-mortal existence, who is our elder brother, the great "I Am," or Jehovah of the Old Testament account, the God of Abraham, Isaac and Jacob, and who became, in the Meridian of Time, the only Begotten of the Father in the flesh, Jesus the Christ, the Redeemer of mankind.

(Alvin R. Dyer, *Who Am I?* [Salt Lake City: Deseret Book, 1966], 124–25.)

SEPTEMBER 20
The Lord Strengthens Us

He giveth power to the faint; and to them that have no might he increaseth strength. . . .

But they that wait upon the Lord shall renew their strength; they shall mount up with wings as eagles; they shall run, and not be weary; and they shall walk, and not faint.

ISAIAH 40:29, 31

See also Ex. 15:2; 2 Sam. 22:33; Ps. 18:2; 2 Ne. 22:2.

Every time they persecute and try to overcome this people, they elevate us, weaken their own hands, and strengthen the hands and arms of this people. And every time they undertake to lessen our number, they increase it. And when they try to destroy the faith and virtue of this people, the Lord strengthens the feeble knees, and confirms the wavering in faith and power in God, in light, and intelligence.

(Brigham Young, *Discourses of Brigham Young* [Salt Lake City: Deseret Book, 1954], 351.)

SEPTEMBER 21
The Lord Hears and Blesses Us

When the poor and needy seek water, and there is none, and their tongue faileth for thirst, I the Lord will hear them, I the God of Israel will not forsake them.

I will open rivers in high places, and fountains in the midst of the valleys: I will make the wilderness a pool of water, and the dry land springs of water.

ISAIAH 41:17–18

See also 2 Kgs. 19:20; 3 Ne. 17:5–10; Ether 1:35.

Miracles are wrought by faith, and the Lord blesses those who have faith in him. He who will not have faith and will not believe until he has proof will not receive the blessings which are promised. The Lord said: "Ask, and it shall be given you; seek and ye shall find; knock, and it shall be opened unto you: For every one that asketh receiveth; and he that seeketh findeth; and to him that knocketh it shall be opened."

(Howard W. Hunter, *The Teachings of Howard W. Hunter* [Salt Lake City: Bookcraft, 1997], 30.)

SEPTEMBER 22
The Lord Reclaims the Lost

And I will bring the blind by a way that they knew not; I will lead them in paths that they have not known: I will make darkness light before them, and crooked things straight. These things will I do unto them, and not forsake them.

ISAIAH 42:16

See also Ps. 23:1; Isa. 40:11; 3 Ne. 10:4–6; D&C 10:65.

People today face the same temptations that have been common throughout history, plus many others that were unknown to earlier generations. However, God will not allow us to be tempted beyond our ability to resist. He does not give us challenges that we cannot surmount. He will not ask more than we can do, but may ask right up to our limits so we can prove ourselves. The Lord will never forsake or abandon anyone. We may abandon him, but he will not abandon us. We never need to feel that we are alone.

(Joseph B. Wirthlin, *Finding Peace in Our Lives* [Salt Lake City: Deseret Book, 1995], 152.)

SEPTEMBER 23

The Lord Forgives the Sins of the Penitent

❦

I, even I, am he that blotteth out thy transgressions
for mine own sake, and will not remember thy sins.

ISAIAH 43:25

See also Isa. 44:21–23; 1 Jn. 1:9; 3 Ne. 13:14–15.

Sometimes it is easier for the Lord not to
remember our sins than it is for us. They become a
cross because we will not do ourselves the favor of
carrying on. "By this ye may know if a man repenteth
of his sins—behold, he will confess them and forsake
them." Can you carry appropriately the cross of forgiveness? Some of us would rather carry a cross than
confess and start anew.

(Marvin J. Ashton, *Be of Good Cheer* [Salt Lake City: Deseret
Book, 1987], 33.)

SEPTEMBER 24
The Lord Will Never Forget Us

Can a woman forget her sucking child, that she should not have compassion on the son of her womb? yea, they may forget, yet will I not forget thee.

Behold, I have graven thee upon the palms of my hands; thy walls are continually before me.

ISAIAH 49:15–16

See also Isa. 49:13.

We may rest assured that the predictions concerning the calamities and judgments which are about to fall upon the wicked, the unbelieving and the unrepentant will all be fulfilled, as will every word and promise which the Lord has spoken to us. But while we warn others, let us not forget ourselves, or our families. Let us look well to our own lives and the conduct and lives of those who belong to our household. If we keep ourselves unspotted from sin, rest assured the Lord will never forget or forsake us.

(John Taylor and George Q. Cannon in James R. Clark, comp., *Messages of the First Presidency of The Church of Jesus Christ of Latter-day Saints* [Salt Lake City: Bookcraft, 1965–75], 3:38.)

SEPTEMBER 25
The Plan of Salvation Is Centered in Christ

And now, behold, I say unto you: This is the plan of salvation unto all men, through the blood of mine Only Begotten, who shall come in the meridian of time.

MOSES 6:62

See also Ps. 27:1; Isa. 45:17.

Of the Christ-centered plan of salvation, Lehi declared, "How great the importance to make these things known unto the inhabitants of the earth." Each portion of the Restoration not only affirms the reality of a redeeming Christ but also informs us that He has set the example for us as to the qualities we are to develop. Each divine disclosure deepens our regard for Him, our exemplar.

Jesus is even described as the Father, because under Elohim's direction he is the Father-Creator of this and other worlds. Furthermore, He is the Father of all who are born again spiritually. When we take upon ourselves His name and covenant to keep His commandments, it is then that we become His sons and daughters, "the children of Christ."

(Neal A. Maxwell, *Men and Women of Christ* [Salt Lake City: Bookcraft, 1991], 37.)

SEPTEMBER 26
The Infinite and Eternal Atonement

For the life of the flesh is in the blood: and I have given it to you upon the altar to make an atonement for your souls: for it is the blood that maketh an atonement for the soul.

LEVITICUS 17:11

See also Isa. 53:6; 63:9; Zech. 9:11; 3 Ne. 27:13–14.

Everything depended on Him—His atoning sacrifice. That was the key. That was the keystone in the arch of the great plan which the Father had brought forth for the eternal life of His sons and daughters. Terrible as it was to face it, and burdensome as it was to realize it, He faced it, He accomplished it, and it was a marvelous and wonderful thing. It is beyond our comprehension, I believe. Nevertheless, we glimpse it in small part and must learn to appreciate it more and more and more.

(Gordon B. Hinckley, *Teachings of Gordon B. Hinckley* [Salt Lake City: Deseret Book, 1997], 30.)

SEPTEMBER 27

Hope in and through the Lord Jesus Christ

Let thy mercy, O Lord, be upon us, according as
we hope in thee.

PSALM 33:22

See also Ps. 42:11; Prov. 10:28; Eccl. 9:4; Joel 3:16; Titus
1:2.

We have a hope in Christ here and now. He died
for our sins. Because of him and his gospel, our sins
are washed away in the waters of baptism; sin and
iniquity are burned out of our souls as though by fire;
and we become clean, have clear consciences, and
gain that peace which passeth understanding.

(Spencer W. Kimball, *The Teachings of Spencer W. Kimball*
[Salt Lake City: Bookcraft, 1982], 22.)

SEPTEMBER 28

Our Souls Are Healed through the Atonement

I said, Lord, be merciful unto me: heal my soul;
for I have sinned against thee.

PSALM 41:4

See also Pss. 103:3; 147:3; Isa. 57:18–19; Jer. 17:14.

How can the atonement of Jesus work in our
lives if there is no repentance? If we do not promptly
remove the slivers of sin and the thorns of carnal
temptation, how can the Lord ever heal our souls?
The Savior said, "Repent of your sins, and be converted, that I may heal you."

(James E. Faust, *Finding Light in a Dark World* [Salt Lake
City: Deseret Book, 1995], 17–18.)

SEPTEMBER 29

Gratitude to our Savior, Jesus Christ

And to stand every morning to thank and praise
the Lord, and likewise at even.

1 CHRONICLES 23:30

See also 2 Sam. 22:50; Pss. 50:14; 95:2; 136:1; Luke 1:47.

Christ's atonement for their individual sins was
entirely beyond the scope of justice—it was an act of
pure mercy. It seems to me that, if possible (particu-
larly since it was an act beyond the power of men to
do for themselves), we owe our Redeemer an even
deeper debt of gratitude for this aspect of his atonement than we do for bringing about the resurrection.

(Marion G. Romney, *Look to God and Live* [Salt Lake City:
Deseret Book, 1971], 98.)

And it shall be unto you for a fringe, that ye may look upon it, and remember all the commandments of the Lord, and do them; and that ye seek not after your own heart and your own eyes, after which ye use to go a whoring:

That ye may remember, and do all my commandments, and be holy unto your God.

NUMBERS 15:39–40

See also 1 Chr.16:12; Ps. 105:5; 1 Cor. 11:2; Mosiah 4:11.

Jesus' responsibility as Advocate, Savior, and Redeemer was foredetermined in premortal realms and fulfilled by His atonement. Your responsibility is to remember, to repent, and to be righteous.

(Russell M. Nelson, *Perfection Pending, and Other Favorite Discourses* [Salt Lake City: Deseret Book, 1998], 157.)

OCTOBER

Who am I, that I should go unto Pharaoh . . .

—EXODUS 3:11

OCTOBER 1
Saviors on Mount Zion

And saviours shall come up on mount Zion to judge the mount of Esau; and the kingdom shall be the Lord's.

OBADIAH 1:21

See also Mal. 4:5–6; D&C 76:73; 128:15.

God is looking upon us, and has called us to be saviors upon Mount Zion. And what does a savior mean? It means a person who saves somebody. Jesus went and preached to the spirits in prison; and he was a savior to that people. When he came to atone for the sins of the world, he was a savior, was he not? Yes. And we are told in the revelations that saviors should stand upon Mount Zion; and the kingdom shall be the Lord's. Would we be saviors if we did not save somebody? I think not. Could we save anyone if we did not build temples? No, we could not; for God would not accept our offerings and sacrifices. Then we came here to be saviors on Mount Zion, and the kingdom is to be the Lord's. Then what shall we do? We will build temples. And what then? Administer in them.

(John Taylor, *The Gospel Kingdom: Selections from the Writings and Discourses of John Taylor* [Salt Lake City: Improvement Era, 1941], 287–88.)

OCTOBER 2
Build up the Kingdom of God

Enlarge the place of thy tent, and let them stretch forth the curtains of thine habitations: spare not, lengthen thy cords, and strengthen thy stakes.

ISAIAH 54:2

See also Isa. 33:20; D&C 115:5–6.

We are here to live, to spread intelligence and knowledge among the people. I am here to school my brethren, to teach my family the way of life, to propagate my species, and to live, if in my power, until sin, iniquity, corruption, hell, and the Devil, and all classes and grades of abominations are driven from the earth. That is my religion and the object of my existence. We are not here merely to prepare to die, and then die; but we are here to live and build up the Kingdom of God on the earth.

(Brigham Young, *Discourses of Brigham Young* [Salt Lake City: Deseret Book, 1954], 88.)

OCTOBER 3
Go Where the Lord Commands

And the Lord shall scatter you among the nations, and ye shall be left few in number among the heathen, whither the Lord shall lead you. . . .

If from thence thou shalt seek the Lord thy God, thou shalt find him, if thou seek him with all thy heart and with all thy soul.

DEUTERONOMY 4:27, 29

See also Isa. 54:2; Luke 22:32; Moro. 10:31; D&C 82:14.

I will go where the Lord and the leaders of His Church want me to go, I will do what they want me to do, I will teach what they want me to teach, and I will strive to become what I should and must become. In the strength of the Lord and through His grace, I know that you and I can be blessed to accomplish all things.

(David A. Bednar, "In the Strength of the Lord," *Ensign*, Nov. 2004, 78.)

Is not this the fast that I have chosen? to loose the bands of wickedness, to undo the heavy burdens, and to let the oppressed go free, and that ye break every yoke?

Is it not to deal thy bread to the hungry, and that thou bring the poor that are cast out to thy house? when thou seest the naked, that thou cover him; and that thou hide not thyself from thine own flesh?

ISAIAH 58:6–7

See also Isa. 58:8–11; Joel 2:12; Alma 5:46; D&C 59:13.

The law of the fast has three great purposes. First, it provides assistance to the needy through the contribution of fast offerings, consisting of the value of meals from which we abstain. Second, a fast is beneficial to us physically. Third, it is to increase humility and spirituality on the part of each individual.

(L. Tom Perry, "The Law of the Fast," *Ensign,* May 1986, 31.)

OCTOBER 5
Blessings of the Fast

But as for me, when they were sick, my clothing was sackcloth: I humbled my soul with fasting; and my prayer returned into mine own bosom.

PSALM 35:13

See also Ezra 8:23; Neh. 1:4; 9:1; Ps. 69:10; Joel 2:12.

The law of the fast is another test. If we merely go without food to supply welfare funds, it is much of the letter, but in real fasting, for spiritual blessings, come self-mastery and increased spirituality.

(Spencer W. Kimball, *The Teachings of Spencer W. Kimball* [Salt Lake City: Bookcraft, 1982], 145.)

OCTOBER 6
Second Coming of the Lord

And I will pour upon the house of David, and upon the inhabitants of Jerusalem, the spirit of grace and of supplications: and they shall look upon me whom they have pierced, and they shall mourn for him, as one mourneth for his only son, and shall be in bitterness for him, as one that is in bitterness for his firstborn.

Zechariah 12:10

See also Ps. 102:16; Isa.63:1–6; Micah 1:3; D&C 38:8.

We believe that his judgments are poured out to bring mankind to a sense of his power and his purposes, that they may repent of their sins and prepare themselves for the second coming of Christ to reign in righteousness upon the earth.

(Joseph F. Smith, *Gospel Doctrine: Selections from the Sermons and Writings of Joseph F. Smith* [Salt Lake City: Deseret Book, 1939], 55.)

OCTOBER 7
The Lord Will Prepare Us to Meet Him

Behold, I have refined thee, but not with silver; I have chosen thee in the furnace of affliction.

ISAIAH 48:10

See also Amos 4:12; Alma 5:28; 34:32; D&C 133:10.

Avoid procrastination. We can say with great accuracy procrastination is an unwholesome blend of doubt and delay. Oft-used words of the Savior such as *ask, seek, knock, go, thrust,* are action words. He would have us use action as we teach and live His principles.

(Marvin J. Ashton, *Be of Good Cheer* [Salt Lake City: Deseret Book, 1987], 61.)

OCTOBER 8

The Millennium—A Time of Peace and Joy

And there shall be mine abode, and it shall be
Zion, which shall come forth out of all the creations
which I have made; and for the space of a thousand
years the earth shall rest.

MOSES 7:64

See also Isa. 65:17–25; Rev. 20:4; D&C 29:11; 77:12.

We believe that if we can establish faith in the
minds of the rising generation, if we can teach the
truth in such a way that our Father's children will
seek him and his influence *first,* that this world will
begin to prepare for the Millennium, when there
will be joy and peace and happiness, and when our
Heavenly Father will establish his kingdom, into
which he has invited every child of his that has been
born into the world.

(George Albert Smith, *The Teachings of George Albert Smith*
[Salt Lake City: Bookcraft, 1996], 152.)

OCTOBER 9
Foreordination—A Call to Serve

Before I formed thee in the belly I knew thee; and before thou camest forth out of the womb I sanctified thee, and I ordained thee a prophet unto the nations.

JEREMIAH 1:5

See also Job 38:7; Eph. 1:4; Alma 13:3–9; Abr. 3:23.

Every man who has a calling to minister to the inhabitants of the world was ordained to that very purpose in the Grand Council of heaven before this world was. I suppose that I was ordained to this very office in that Grand Council.

(*History of the Church* 6:364–65.)

OCTOBER 10
Serve in the Strength of the Lord

But the Lord said unto me, Say not, I am a child: for thou shalt go to all that I shall send thee, and whatsoever I command thee thou shalt speak.

Be not afraid of their faces: for I am with thee to deliver thee, saith the Lord.

JEREMIAH 1:7–8

See also Jer. 1:9; Ps. 28:7–8.

King Benjamin was truly conscious that God is the loving Father of all men; he taught his people, "When you are in the service of your fellow beings ye are in the service of your God!" The Lord is the strength of all who serve Him, and the praise of them that love to do His will. Herein is wisdom.

(George Reynolds and Janne M. Sjodahl, *Commentary on the Book of Mormon* [Salt Lake City: Deseret Book, 1955–1961], 2:44.)

OCTOBER 11

Endure in the Face of Opposition

Then spake the priests and the prophets unto the princes and to all the people, saying, This man is worthy to die; for he hath prophesied against this city, as ye have heard with your ears.

Then spake Jeremiah unto all the princes and to all the people, saying, The Lord sent me to prophesy against this house and against this city all the words that ye have heard.

JEREMIAH 26:11–12

See also Matt. 10:22; Heb. 6:15; 2 Ne. 31:20; D&C 63:20.

The days of tribulation are fast approaching, and the time to test the fidelity of the Saints has come. Rumor with her ten thousand tongues is diffusing her uncertain sounds in almost every ear; but in these times of sore trial, let the Saints be patient and see the salvation of God. Those who cannot endure persecution, and stand in the day of affliction, cannot stand in the day when the Son of God shall burst the veil, and appear in all the glory of his Father, with all the holy angels.

(*History of the Church* 1:468.)

OCTOBER 12
Strengthened by the Word of God

Then the Lord put forth his hand, and touched my mouth. And the Lord said unto me, Behold, I have put my words in thy mouth.

JEREMIAH 1:9

See also Jer. 15:16; 2 Ne. 32:3; Alma 31:5; D&C 84:85–88.

Through reading the scriptures, we can gain the assurance of the Spirit that that which we read has come of God for the enlightenment, blessing, and joy of his children.

I urge our people everywhere to read the scriptures more—to study all of them together. . . . for a harmony of understanding in order to bring their precepts into our lives.

May the Lord bless each of us to feast upon his holy word and to draw from it that strength, that peace, that knowledge "which passeth all understanding," as he has promised.

(Gordon B. Hinckley, "He Is at Peace," *Ensign,* Dec. 1985, 45.)

OCTOBER 13
Becoming Like the Lord

O house of Israel, cannot I do with you as this potter? saith the Lord. Behold, as the clay is in the potter's hand, so are ye in mine hand, O house of Israel.

JEREMIAH 18:6

See also Mosiah 3:19; 3 Ne. 21:10; D&C 100:1–2.

Men and women who turn their lives over to God will discover that He can make a lot more out of their lives than they can. He will deepen their joys, expand their vision, quicken their minds, strengthen their muscles, lift their spirits, multiply their blessings, increase their opportunities, comfort their souls, raise up friends, and pour out peace. Whoever will lose his life in the service of God will find eternal.

(Ezra Taft Benson, *The Teachings of Ezra Taft Benson* [Salt Lake City: Bookcraft, 1988], 361.)

OCTOBER 14
Prophets Preach Repentance

***

Now therefore go to, speak to the men of Judah, and to the inhabitants of Jerusalem, saying, Thus saith the Lord; Behold, I frame evil against you, and devise a device against you: return ye now every one from his evil way, and make your ways and your doings good.

JEREMIAH 18:11

See also 2 Kgs. 17:13; Neh. 9:30; Ezek. 3:19.

The lines are being more sharply drawn, every day of our lives, as never before; and we can look over the world and know for a surety the distinction between the peace of the gospel of Jesus Christ and the conflict and envy so manifest in daily strife. We must preach repentance, as the Prophet Joseph through inspiration declares in so many of his revelations, and preach, too, the restoration of the gospel of Jesus Christ.

(David O. McKay, *Gospel Ideals: Selections from the Discourses of David O. McKay* [Salt Lake City: Improvement Era, 1953], 20.)

OCTOBER 15
Beware of Worldliness

And the Lord said unto Satan, Hast thou considered my servant Job, that there is none like him in the earth, a perfect and an upright man, one that feareth God, and escheweth evil?

JOB 1:8

See also 1 Chr. 16:26; Jer. 2:5; 1 Pet. 4:3; Alma 1:32.

If, after the expiration of fifty years, we as a community do not stand in that high relationship to God that we could wish, the fault is not in the Lord, it is not for the lack of information placed before us, but that lack is in ourselves; it arises from our ignorance or neglect, or from a desire, peradventure, to serve the spirit of the world instead of the Spirit of God.

(Lorenzo Snow, *The Teachings of Lorenzo Snow* [Salt Lake City: Bookcraft, 1984], 131.)

OCTOBER 16
The Latter-day Gathering of Israel

❦

And I will gather the remnant of my flock out of all countries whither I have driven them, and will bring them again to their folds; and they shall be fruitful and increase.

JEREMIAH 23:3

See also Jer. 16:14–16; 29:14; 2 Ne. 21:12; D&C 45:25.

From the beginning of the great Latter-Day work men had their attention directed to the gathering of Israel and the establishment of Zion and Jerusalem as a part of the purposes of God to be accomplished in the work. The angel Moroni on the occasion of his first visit to the Prophet Joseph, quoted a number of Old Testament scriptures referring to the Lord's promises concerning the redemption of Judah and Jerusalem; also concerning the gathering of Israel from all the lands whither they had been driven.

(*History of the Church* 2:xxvi–xxvii.)

OCTOBER 17
Shepherds of Israel

And I will set up shepherds over them which shall feed them: and they shall fear no more, nor be dismayed, neither shall they be lacking, saith the Lord.

JEREMIAH 23:4

See also Ezek. 33:7; Matt. 20:26; Jarom 1:7.

As the Church moves into the challenges of the last decades of this century, the need for leadership through the wards and stakes of Zion will increase dramatically. What is needed is not just young people of training and skill, but rather we will need a generation of great faith, those who have learned discipline and discipleship. What will be needed is a generation who understand not only how to organize a ward but also how to build faith, how to sustain the weak and faltering, and how to defend the truth. What is needed is a generation whose glory comes from their capacity to comprehend light and truth, who can with that light and truth then enlarge their capacity to love and to serve.

(Howard W. Hunter, *The Teachings of Howard W. Hunter* [Salt Lake City: Bookcraft, 1997], 122.)

OCTOBER 18
Missionaries in the Latter Days

❦

Behold, I will send for many fishers, saith the Lord, and they shall fish them; and after will I send for many hunters, and they shall hunt them from every mountain, and from every hill, and out of the holes of the rocks.

JEREMIAH 16:16

See also Isa. 52:7; 61:1; Jer. 3:14; D&C 15:6; 18:15–16.

We need more missionaries. But we also need better-prepared missionaries coming out of the wards and branches and homes where they know and love the Book of Mormon. A great challenge and day of preparation is at hand for missionaries to meet and teach with the Book of Mormon. We need missionaries to match our message.

(Ezra Taft Benson, *The Teachings of Ezra Taft Benson* [Salt Lake City: Bookcraft, 1988], 192.)

OCTOBER 19
Covenants

But this shall be the covenant that I will make with the house of Israel; After those days, saith the Lord, I will put my law in their inward parts, and write it in their hearts; and will be their God, and they shall be my people.

JEREMIAH 31:33

See also Ps. 19:7; 51:13; Isa. 60:3; Ezek. 18:31; Alma 5:14.

Covenants . . . are essential for our eternal progression. Step-by-step, He tutors us to become like Him by enlisting us in His work. At baptism we covenant to love Him with all our hearts and love our sisters and brothers as ourselves. In the temple we further covenant to be obedient, selfless, faithful, honorable, charitable. We covenant to make sacrifices and consecrate all that we have. Forged through priesthood authority, our kept covenants bring blessings to fill our cups to overflowing. . . . Making covenants is the expression of a willing heart; keeping covenants, the expression of a faithful heart.

(Bonnie D. Parkin, "With Holiness of Heart," *Ensign,* Nov. 2002, 103.)

OCTOBER 20
Saints of the Latter Days

And many people shall go and say, Come ye, and let us go up to the mountain of the Lord, to the house of the God of Jacob; and he will teach us of his ways, and we will walk in his paths: for out of Zion shall go forth the law, and the word of the Lord from Jerusalem.

ISAIAH 2:3

See also Ps. 50:5; Dan. 7:18; Rom. 1:7; Mosiah 3:19.

Christian virtues and godly conduct abound in the lives of the Lord's people. . . . Where these heaven-patterned virtues are, there are the true saints; where these are not, true religion has not taken hold of the souls of men, however devout they may otherwise appear to be.

(Bruce R. McConkie, *Doctrinal New Testament Commentary* [Salt Lake City: Bookcraft, 1965–1973], 3:304.)

OCTOBER 21
Hearken to the Word of God

The Lord thy God will raise up unto thee a Prophet from the midst of thee, of thy brethren, like unto me; unto him ye shall hearken.

DEUTERONOMY 18:15

See also Ps. 19:7; Isa. 8:20; 1 Ne. 15:24–25; Alma 49:30.

These commandments you will not find grievous or hard to bear. If you will hearken to my word you shall find peace and eternal joy, and eternal freedom shall be given you, for my word is truth and it is the truth which makes you free. You may refuse to obey my voice and you may rebel against my law, for this power is in you; but remember if you do, you shall bring upon you the second death, which is banishment from my presence.

(Joseph Fielding Smith, *The Way to Perfection* [Salt Lake City: Genealogical Society of Utah, 1949], 182.)

OCTOBER 22
Trust in the Lord

Thus saith the Lord; Cursed be the man that trusteth in man, and maketh flesh his arm, and whose heart departeth from the Lord. . . .

Blessed is the man that trusteth in the Lord, and whose hope the Lord is.

JEREMIAH 17:5, 7

See also 2 Sam. 22:3; 1 Chr. 5:20; 2 Chr. 13:18; Pss. 22:4.

Teach all men to trust in God and not in man, and do works meet for repentance. Again, teach all men that God is a God of the living and not of the dead. Finally, whatever you do, do it with an eye single to the glory of God. You are the light of the world in matters of pure religion, and many souls may be required at your hands. Let the idea not leave you, that not only the eyes of the world, but the eyes of the angels and of God are upon you.

(*History of the Church* 1:280–81.)

OCTOBER 23
Serve Willingly and Faithfully

Remember that thou magnify his work, which men behold.

JOB 36:24

See also Deut. 6:13; 10:12; 11:13–15; 1 Kgs. 12:7.

We counsel you to accept callings in the Church and to serve faithfully in the positions to which you are called. Serve one another. Magnify your callings. As you do so, you will be the means of blessing others and you will increase in spirituality.

(Ezra Taft Benson, *The Teachings of Ezra Taft Benson* [Salt Lake City: Bookcraft, 1988], 454.)

OCTOBER 24
All Have a Call to Serve

❧

They helped every one his neighbour; and every one said to his brother, Be of good courage.

ISAIAH 41:6

See also Judg. 2:7; 2 Ne. 6:2; Alma 42:31; D&C 4:3.

We invite all to serve the Savior and walk in His paths straightway. There is an urgency for all of us who have this knowledge of His divinity to act upon it without hesitation or delay. The time is now. . . . Not tomorrow, not when we get ready, not when it is convenient—but "this day," straightway, choose whom you will serve. He who invites us to follow will always be out in front of us with His Spirit and influence setting the pace. He has charted and marked the course, opened the gates, and shown the way. He has invited us to come unto Him, and the best time to enjoy His companionship is straightway. We can best get on the course and stay on the course by doing as Jesus did—make a total commitment to do the will of His Father.

(Marvin J. Ashton, *Be of Good Cheer* [Salt Lake City: Deseret Book, 1987], 56.)

OCTOBER 25
Righteous Leadership

Therefore, ye shepherds, hear the word of the Lord.

Ezekiel 34:7

See also Num. 11:17; Jacob 1:19; Mosiah 23:14; 3 Ne. 27:27.

May I also express my gratitude to you fathers and husbands assembled this evening. We look to you to give righteous leadership in your home and families and, with your companions and the mothers of your children, to lead your families back to our Eternal Father.

Now God bless our wonderful mothers. We pray for you. We sustain you. We honor you as you bear, nourish, train, teach, and love for eternity. I promise you the blessings of heaven and "all that [the] Father hath" as you magnify the noblest calling of all—a mother in Zion.

(Ezra Taft Benson, *Come, Listen to a Prophet's Voice* [Salt Lake City: Deseret Book, 1990], 37.)

OCTOBER 26

Christ Is Our True Shepherd

But his bow abode in strength, and the arms of his hands were made strong by the hands of the mighty God of Jacob; (from thence is the shepherd, the stone of Israel.)

GENESIS 49:24

See also Pss. 23; 80:1–3; John 10:11; Heb. 13:20; 1 Ne. 22:25.

Jesus, our Shepherd, has "marked the path and led the way, And ev'ry point defines." His clearly defined footprints are easy to see. They are pressed distinctly and deeply into the soil of the second estate, deeply and distinctly because of the enormous weight which pressed down upon Him, including the awful burden of all of our individual sins.

(Neal A. Maxwell, *The Neal A. Maxwell Quote Book* [Salt Lake City: Bookcraft, 1997], 34.)

OCTOBER 27
Repentance and Forgiveness

Again, when the wicked man turneth away from his wickedness that he hath committed, and doeth that which is lawful and right, he shall save his soul alive.

EZEKIEL 18:27

See also Ezek. 18:28–32; Luke 24:47; Enos 1:5.

King Benjamin's teaching had a miraculous effect. Gratitude for what they had led to faith unto repentance. That led to forgiveness. That produced new gratitude. And then King Benjamin taught that, if we can remember and so remain grateful, we will retain a remission of our sins through all the losses and the gains of life.

(Henry B. Eyring, *To Draw Closer to God: A Collection of Discourses* [Salt Lake City: Deseret Book, 1997], 77.)

Consequences of Sin

But when the righteous turneth away from his righteousness, and committeth iniquity, and doeth according to all the abominations that the wicked man doeth, shall he live? All his righteousness that he hath done shall not be mentioned: in his trespass that he hath trespassed, and in his sin that he hath sinned, in them shall he die.

EZEKIEL 18:24

See also Gen. 4:7; Deut. 24:16; Ps. 51:1–3; Mosiah 2:33.

The painful consequences of sin were purposely put in His plan of happiness by a compassionate Father in Heaven so that you need not follow that tragic path in life. A sinner will not only suffer in this life, but sins that have not been forgiven through true repentance will cause anguish beyond the veil. . . . In fact, each of us needs consistently to repent and obey so that the gift of the Savior will satisfy the demands of justice for even our small errors of commission or omission.

The Savior will take upon Himself the consequences of your sins as you repent now. If that is not done, in time you will have to suffer for them yourself.

(Richard G. Scott, "To Be Free of Heavy Burdens," *Ensign*, Nov. 2002, 86.)

OCTOBER 29
Two Witnesses of Christ

Say unto them, Thus saith the Lord God; Behold, I will take the stick of Joseph, which is in the hand of Ephraim, and the tribes of Israel his fellows, and will put them with him, even with the stick of Judah, and make them one stick, and they shall be one in mine hand.

EZEKIEL 37:19

See also Isa. 29:4; Ps. 85:11; 2 Cor. 13:1; 1 Ne. 13:38–42.

All scripture comes from God; all scripture is true; and every divine word accords with every other word from the same heavenly source. The Bible bears witness of the Book of Mormon, and the Book of Mormon testifies of the Bible. They are both true; they both came from God; neither is false, and both are accepted by true believers. Those who believe one believe the other, and those who reject one reject, in a very real sense the other. Mormon put it just this bluntly: If ye believe the Bible, ye will believe the Book of Mormon also.

(Bruce R. McConkie, *A New Witness for the Articles of Faith* [Salt Lake City: Deseret Book, 1985], 394.)

OCTOBER 30
House of the Lord

Therefore thus saith the Lord; I am returned to Jerusalem with mercies: my house shall be built in it, saith the Lord of hosts, and a line shall be stretched forth upon Jerusalem.

ZECHARIAH 1:16

See also 1 Chr. 22:6; 28:6; 2 Ne. 5:16; Jacob 1:17.

We also now have the temple and all that means in our learning experience. Interestingly, not only spiritual but also what we think of as temporal learning develops in us through the temple experience. The instruction given in the endowment provides a firm perspective, a point of reference by which a person may gauge all his learning and wisdom, both spiritual and temporal; by which he may gather things together, determine their true meaning and significance, and fit them into their proper places.

(Boyd K. Packer, *The Holy Temple* [Salt Lake City: Bookcraft, 1980], 45.)

OCTOBER 31
Glory of the Lord in the Temple

And the glory of the Lord came into the house by
the way of the gate whose prospect is toward the east.

So the spirit took me up, and brought me into the
inner court; and, behold, the glory of the Lord filled
the house.

EZEKIEL 43:4–5

See also Ex. 25:8; 29:43; 40:34; D&C 84:32; 97:15.

The most important reason for the building of the
Kirtland Temple was that there might be a sacred place
dedicated to the name of the Lord to which his ancient
servants might come, as the Savior did himself, to restore
the covenants and authorities of the Holy Priesthood. . . .
First of all came the Savior who accepted the house, and
the temple was filled with the glory of the Lord. It was
in that temple that Moses came, committing the keys
of the gathering of Israel. Elias who lived in the days of
Abraham, committed the keys of the dispensation of
Abraham; and Elijah came, fulfilling the promise of the
Lord through Malachi, turning the hearts of the fathers
to the children and the children to their fathers.

(Joseph Fielding Smith, *Answers to Gospel Questions* [Salt
Lake City: Deseret Book, 1957–1966], 4:192.)

NOVEMBER

*The Lord our God be with us, as he
was with our fathers . . .*

—1 KINGS 8:57

NOVEMBER 1

The Lord Dwells in the Temple

But the Lord is in his holy temple: let all the earth keep silence before him.

HABAKKUK 2:20

See also 2 Sam. 7:5; Ps. 11:4; D&C 110:7; 124:40.

Temples are the most sacred places of worship on earth where sacred ordinances are performed—ordinances that pertain to salvation and exaltation in the kingdom of God. Each one is literally a house of the Lord—a place where he and his Spirit may dwell, where he may come or send others to confer priesthood blessings and to give revelation to his people.

(David B. Haight, *A Light unto the World* [Salt Lake City: Deseret Book, 1997], 44.)

NOVEMBER 2
Laws and Commandments of the Lord

And if they be ashamed of all that they have done, shew them the form of the house, and the fashion thereof, and the goings out thereof, and the comings in thereof, and all the forms thereof, and all the ordinances thereof, and all the forms thereof, and all the laws thereof: and write it in their sight, that they may keep the whole form thereof, and all the ordinances thereof, and do them.

EZEKIEL 43:11

See also Deut. 6:17, 24; 33:4; Matt. 22:37–40; D&C 29:35.

To insure progress the powers of man must be exercised for the achievement of the great objective of existence. He must become by every act more and more like the Lord of heaven. That is the highest hope and highest conception of joy by every thinking person. In a small degree this is attainable by man, through strict obedience to the laws of the Lord.

(John A. Widtsoe, *Evidences and Reconciliations* [Salt Lake City: Improvement Era], 182.)

NOVEMBER 3
Temple Worthiness

And the Lord said unto him, I have heard thy prayer and thy supplication, that thou has made before me: I have hallowed this house, which thou hast built, to put my name there for ever; and mine eyes and mine heart shall be there perpetually.

1 KINGS 9:3

See also Ps. 24:3–4; Dan. 11:31; Matt. 21:13; D&C 93:35.

The Lord desires that his people be a temple-motivated people. It would be the deepest desire of my heart to have every member of the Church be temple worthy. I would hope that every adult member would be worthy of—and carry—a current temple recommend, even if proximity to a temple does not allow immediate or frequent use of it. Let us be a temple-attending and a temple-loving people.

(Howard W. Hunter, *The Teachings of Howard W. Hunter* [Salt Lake City: Bookcraft, 1997], 239.)

NOVEMBER 4
Blessings of the Righteous

A faithful man shall abound with blessings: but he that maketh haste to be rich shall not be innocent.

PROVERBS 28:20

See also Pss. 2:12; 24:4–5; D&C 41:1.

But God's love and mercy was again to be manifested. Men were not to be left without the knowledge of the essentials of the plan of salvation, nor without opportunity to enjoy the blessings of a righteous life under the reign of the God-given Gospel plan.

(J. Reuben Clark, *On the Way to Immortality and Eternal Life* [Salt Lake City: Deseret Book, 1949], 107–08.)

NOVEMBER 5
Just Shall Live by Faith

Behold, his soul which is lifted up is not upright in him: but the just shall live by his faith.

HABAKKUK 2:4

See also 2 Chr. 20:20; Isa. 43:10; Dan. 6:23; Matt. 21:21.

If there is any one thing you and I need in this world it is faith, that dynamic, powerful, marvelous element by which, as Paul declared, the very worlds were framed. . . . Faith—the kind of faith that moves one to get on his knees and plead with the Lord and then get on his feet and go to work—is an asset beyond compare.

(Gordon B. Hinckley, *Teachings of Gordon B. Hinckley* [Salt Lake City: Deseret Book, 1997], 186.)

NOVEMBER 6
Stand for Truth and Righteousness

But Daniel purposed in his heart that he would not defile himself with the portion of the king's meat, nor with the wine which he drank: therefore he requested of the prince of the eunuchs that he might not defile himself.

DANIEL 1:8

See also 1 Sam. 12:20.

All Latter-day Saints . . . provided they are true to their name, to their calling and to their understanding of the gospel, are people who stand for truth and for honor, for virtue and for purity of life, for honesty in business and in religion; people who stand for God and for his righteousness, for God's truth and his work in the earth, which aims, for the salvation of the children of men.

(Joseph F. Smith, *Gospel Doctrine: Selections from the Sermons and Writings of Joseph F. Smith* [Salt Lake City: Deseret Book, 1939], 72.)

NOVEMBER 7
Resisting the Influences of the World

I have sinned: for I have transgressed the commandment of the Lord, and thy words: because I feared the people, and obeyed their voice.

1 SAMUEL 15:24

See also Ex. 23:2; Gal. 1:10; 2 Ne. 8:7.

We not only have this warfare continually, day by day, within ourselves, but we also have an outside influence or pressure to resist. Both the religious and the political world have influences to contend against that very much resemble each other; they are more or less exercised, governed and controlled by surrounding influences. We, Latter-day Saints, have an influence of this kind to contend against.

(Brigham Young, *Discourses of Brigham Young* [Salt Lake City: Deseret Book, 1954], 51.)

NOVEMBER 8
Worship God Only

Blessed be the name of my God, for his Spirit hath not altogether withdrawn from me, or else where is thy glory, for it is darkness unto me? And I can judge between thee and God; for God said unto me: Worship God, for him only shalt thou serve.

MOSES 1:15

See also Ex. 20:3; Pss. 95:6; 99:9; Matt. 4:10; 2 Ne. 25:29.

Worship often includes actions, but true worship always involves a particular attitude of mind.

The attitude of worship evokes the deepest feelings of allegiance, adoration, and awe. Worship combines love and reverence in a state of devotion that draws our spirits closer to God. President Spencer W. Kimball said that the reason God commanded us to worship him is that this would bring us closer to him.

Jesus taught that we should worship the Father "in spirit and in truth."

(Dallin H. Oaks, *Pure in Heart* [Salt Lake City: Bookcraft, 1988], 125.)

NOVEMBER 9
Keep the Commandments

Ye shall diligently keep the commandments of the Lord your God, and his testimonies, and his statutes, which he hath commanded thee.

DEUTERONOMY 6:17

See also Duet. 10:13; John 14:15; 1 Ne. 22:31; Mosiah 2:22.

It is not position, it is not education that gives the Spirit of God; but it is keeping the commandments of Almighty God and being lowly in heart and desiring to fulfill the commandments of God in our daily walk and conversation. I bear witness to you here today that no man has ever fallen in this Church, and no man ever will fail in this Church, who is honest in his heart, honest in the payment of his tithes and offerings, who obeys the Word of Wisdom, who attends to his family prayers and his secret prayers, and who attends to his quorum meetings. No man will fail who is doing his duty in this Church. But Satan has power over those who become selfish and sordid and set their hearts upon the things of the earth and fail to render thanks in all things unto God.

(Heber J. Grant, *Gospel Standards: Selections from the Sermons and Writings of Heber J. Grant* [Salt Lake City: Improvement Era, 1981], 44.)

NOVEMBER 10
The Commandment to Pray

Wherefore, thou shalt do all that thou doest in the name of the Son, and thou shalt repent and call upon God in the name of the Son forevermore.

MOSES 5:8

See also Gen. 21:33; 25:22; 1 Thess. 5:17; Mosiah 26:39.

Prayer is clearly a commandment, and we are even asked to urge others in the Church to pray. It is likewise clear that there are different types of prayer—prayers of adoration, of appreciation, of confession, and of petition. . . . Prayer, in fact, is to be a reflection of our attitude toward God and life. In this sense, we can always be praying. . . . There are no Christlike prayers, however, that do not include, as did the Lord's Prayer, deep expressions of gratitude and appreciation to our Father in heaven along with a submittal to Him.

(Neal A. Maxwell, *All These Things Shall Give Thee Experience* [Salt Lake City: Deseret Book, 1979], 92–93.)

NOVEMBER 11
Obedience Brings the Blessings of the Lord

And when he came to the den, he cried with a lamentable voice unto Daniel: and the king spake and said to Daniel, O Daniel, servant of the living God, is thy God, whom thou servest continually, able to deliver thee from the lions?

Then said Daniel unto the king, O king, live for ever.

My God hath sent his angel, and hath shut the lions' mouths, that they have not hurt me: forasmuch as before him innocency was found in me; and also before thee, O king, have I done no hurt.

DANIEL 6:20–22

See also Isa. 1:19; Rev. 22:14; D&C 58:2; 93:28.

For a living Heavenly Father has plotted our course and provided an unfailing map—*obedience.*

His revealed word vividly describes the blessings that obedience brings and the inevitable heartache and despair that accompany the traveler who detours along the forbidden pathways of sin and error.

(Thomas S. Monson, *Be Your Best Self* [Salt Lake City: Deseret Book, 1979], 102.)

NOVEMBER 12
Courage

Go, gather together all the Jews that are present in Shushan, and fast ye for me, and neither eat nor drink three days, night or day: I also and my maidens will fast likewise; and so will I go in unto the king, which is not according to the law: and if I perish, I perish.

ESTHER 4:16

See also Duet. 31:6; Josh. 1:7; 1 Chr. 28:20; Alma 56:45.

It is my testimony that we are facing difficult times. We must be courageously obedient. My witness is that we will be called upon to prove our spiritual stamina, for the days ahead will be filled with affliction and difficulty. But with the assuring comfort of a personal relationship with the Savior, we will be given a calming courage.

(James E. Faust, *To Reach Even unto You* [Salt Lake City: Deseret Book, 1980], 111.)

NOVEMBER 13
Revelation

Surely the Lord God will do nothing, but he revealeth his secret unto his servants the prophets.

AMOS 3:7

See also Deut. 29:29; Matt. 16:16; 1 Cor. 2:10; 2 Ne. 28:30.

No person received knowledge, only upon the principle of revelation, that is, by having something revealed to them. "Do you have the revelations of the Lord Jesus Christ?" I will leave that for others to judge. If the Lord requires anything of this people, and speaks through me, I will tell them of it; but if he does not, still we all live by the principle of revelation.

(Brigham Young, *Discourses of Brigham Young* [Salt Lake City: Deseret Book, 1954], 39.)

NOVEMBER 14
Beware of a Hard Heart

Wherefore then do ye harden your hearts, as the Egyptians and Pharaoh hardened their hearts? when he had wrought wonderfully among them, did they not let the people go, and they departed?

1 SAMUEL 6:6

See also Deut. 15:7; 2 Chr. 36:13; John 12:40; Mosiah 3:15.

Hardness of heart first comes in the form of forgetfulness, and one consequence of stiffneckedness is an unwillingness or inability to look back at life's lessons. When an individual or a people can no longer be stirred up to remembrance, they soon become "past feeling" as well.

(Neal A. Maxwell, *Lord, Increase Our Faith* [Salt Lake City: Bookcraft, 1994], 103.)

NOVEMBER 15
Gossip

The words of a talebearer are as wounds, and they go down into the innermost parts of the belly.

PROVERBS 18:8

See also Ex. 20:16; Lev. 19:16; Ps. 34:13; Prov. 26:20.

There is a wonderful field in the organizations of the Church for the cultivation of all the virtues of the human heart . . . to lift up and not cast down; to encourage and not to repress; to dispense joy, and to drown sorrow; to refrain their lips from slander and backbiting, and, by sweet temper and kind words, to unfold the better side of human nature; to mind their own business, and not to unduly criticise, and not to find fault, nor to delight in tale-bearing, scandal, envy, and gossip.

This advice heeded, our social ethics would soon show wonderful improvement.

(Joseph F. Smith, *Gospel Doctrine: Selections from the Sermons and Writings of Joseph F. Smith* [Salt Lake City: Deseret Book, 1939], 113.)

NOVEMBER 16
Seeking Answers to Our Questions

And Judah gathered themselves together, to ask help of the Lord: even out of all the cities of Judah they came to seek the Lord.

2 Chronicles 20:4

See also Jer. 50:4–5; Zech. 10:1; Matt. 7:7.

Remember that when you begin to truly seek answers to prayer, there will be forces that will do all in their power to stop you. So don't be surprised when opposition comes; in fact, you should expect it from the beginning. Then, when difficulties really descend upon you and you reach your bleakest moment, you have the opportunity to discover how much faith you really do have.

(Gene R. Cook, *Receiving Answers to Our Prayers* [Salt Lake City: Deseret Book, 1996], 154.)

NOVEMBER 17
The Kingdom of God to Roll Forth

Forasmuch as thou sawest that the stone was cut out of the mountain without hands, and that it brake in pieces the iron, the brass, the clay, the silver, and the gold; the great God hath made known to the king what shall come to pass hereafter: and the dream is certain, and the interpretation thereof sure.

DANIEL 2:45

See also Isa. 9:7; 11:12; Dan. 2:35; 4:3; 7:14.

We will build up the kingdom of God, and roll forth the little stone that Daniel saw cut out of the mountain without hands, and roll forth until it filled the whole earth. For this is the very way that God destines to build up His kingdom in the last days.

(*History of the Church* 3:180–81.)

NOVEMBER 18

The Church in the Latter Days

And in the days of these kings shall the God of heaven set up a kingdom, which shall never be destroyed: and the kingdom shall not be left to other people, but it shall break in pieces and consume all these kingdoms, and it shall stand for ever.

DANIEL 2:44

See also Isa. 2:3; D&C 35:27; 50:35; 82:24.

One of the grand and glorious promises of the Lord when He restored His Church in the latter days was that His Church should never again be taken from the earth nor given to another people. From the very beginning of the Church in this dispensation, detractors, critics, and apostates have ridiculed our practices, misrepresented our doctrines, and slandered our leaders. But the Church has continued to prosper according to the destiny proclaimed by our Heavenly Father.

(Ezra Taft Benson, *The Teachings of Ezra Taft Benson* [Salt Lake City: Bookcraft, 1988], 113.)

NOVEMBER 19
Building up the Kingdom in the Latter Days

How beautiful upon the mountains are the feet of him that bringeth good tidings, that publisheth peace; that bringeth good tidings of good, that publisheth salvation; that saith unto Zion, Thy God reigneth!

ISAIAH 52:7

See also Mormon 9:22; D&C 1:4; 62:5; 88:81; 90:11.

Every person who is called of God to preach the gospel and build up his kingdom in the latter days is but an echo of Joseph Smith. The latter-day Twelve "are called to go unto all the world" and "to preach my gospel unto every creature," the Lord says. . . . They all preach the same gospel and administer the same ordinances, and are endowed with the same power. To all his servants the Lord says: "You shall"—it is mandatory—"declare the things which have been revealed to my servant, Joseph Smith, Jun."

(Bruce R. McConkie, *The Millennial Messiah: The Second Coming of the Son of Man* [Salt Lake City: Deseret Book, 1982], 334–35.)

NOVEMBER 20
Zion

And it came to pass that Enoch talked with the Lord; and he said unto the Lord: Surely Zion shall dwell in safety forever. But the Lord said unto Enoch: Zion have I blessed, but the residue of the people have I cursed.

Moses 7:20

See also Pss. 102:13; 132:13; Isa. 1:27; 2:3; 51:3.

Zion is the name given by the Lord to his saints; it is the name by which the Lord's people are always identified. Of the saints in Enoch's day the record says: *"And the Lord called his people ZION, because they were of one heart and one mind, and dwelt in righteousness; and there was no poor among them." "This is Zion—THE PURE IN HEART,"* he said in this day. Thus The Church of Jesus Christ of Latter-day Saints is Zion. Joining the Church is becoming a citizen of Zion.

(Bruce R. McConkie, *Mormon Doctrine* [Salt Lake City: Bookcraft, 1966], 854.)

NOVEMBER 21
A Zion People

For there shall be a day, that the watchmen upon the mount Ephraim shall cry, Arise ye, and let us go up to Zion unto the Lord our God.

For thus saith the Lord; Sing with gladness for Jacob, and shout among the chief of the nations: publish ye, praise ye, and say, O Lord, save thy people, the remnant of Israel.

JEREMIAH 31:6–7

See also Pss. 48:2; 87:2; Isa. 30:19; 4 Ne. 1:15–16.

Only a Zion people can bring in a Zion society. And as the Zion people increase, so we will be able to incorporate more of the principles of Zion until we have a people prepared to receive the Lord.

(Ezra Taft Benson, *The Teachings of Ezra Taft Benson* [Salt Lake City: Bookcraft, 1988], 124.)

NOVEMBER 22
Avoid Contention

Only by pride cometh contention.

PROVERBS 13:10

See also Prov. 22:10; Mosiah 4:14; 3 Ne. 11:29; 4 Ne. 1:2, 15.

The world's way is often contentious. Latter-day Saints should avoid contention because it separates them from the Lord and his Spirit. The Lord's way is harmony and unity and oneness.

(Dallin H. Oaks, *The Lord's Way* [Salt Lake City: Deseret Book, 1991], 12–13.)

NOVEMBER 23
Teach and Testify of Christ

If thy children will keep my covenant and my testimony that I shall teach them, their children shall also sit upon thy throne for evermore.

PSALM 132:12

See also Job 19:25; Ps. 19:7; 2 Ne. 25:23, 26; Jarom 1:11.

Above all, teach the gospel of Jesus Christ with power and authority and continue to bear witness of the divine mission of our Lord and Master, Jesus Christ.

And to all who are honest in heart and who are sincere seekers after truth, we bear our solemn witness that "through the Atonement of Christ, all mankind may be saved, by obedience to the laws and ordinances of the Gospel," as administered by authorized servants who hold the keys of salvation for both the living and the dead.

(Harold B. Lee, *Stand Ye in Holy Places* [Salt Lake City: Deseret Book, 1974], 88.)

NOVEMBER 24
A Day of Thanksgiving

O give thanks unto the Lord; for he is good: for his mercy endureth for ever.

PSALM 136:1

See also Lev. 7:12; 22:29; Ps. 147:7; 1 Thes. 5:18.

There is one day or more in almost every nation that is set apart for the observance of the anniversary of some great event—an occasion for national pride, a day of remembrance, of thanksgiving, of celebration. It may be the birthday of a nation, or of a patriot, the anniversary of a great victory or triumph of a great cause. It is fitting and proper that we should have such days, "lest we forget."

(Hugh B. Brown, *The Eternal Quest* [Salt Lake City: Bookcraft, 1956], 387.)

NOVEMBER 25
Feasting upon the Word

Thy word is a lamp unto my feet, and a light unto my path.

PSALM 119:105

See also Josh. 8:34; 2 Kgs. 23:2; Rom. 15:4; 2 Ne. 32:3.

The word of God is all around us. We have his precious word in the scriptures. The Lord has told us the plain and precious truths that will lead us back to him. He has commanded us to read them, to feast upon the word. We must feast upon his word in order to understand our responsibilities. We can't just nibble.

Elder J. Richard Clarke has written, "The holy scriptures are the word of God. If we are to know God, we must read His words, for therein He stands revealed to the honest heart."

(Joseph B. Wirthlin, *Finding Peace in Our Lives* [Salt Lake City: Deseret Book, 1995], 164.)

NOVEMBER 26
Understanding the Scriptures

So they read in the book in the law of God distinctly, and gave the sense, and caused them to understand the reading.

NEHEMIAH 8:8

See also Ps. 119:130, 169; Prov. 2:6; 1 Ne. 19:23; 3 Ne. 10:14.

You and I have the responsibility to learn the word of God, to understand the word of God, and then to live His word. By so doing, we will find that we have learned and accepted the truth. The Prophet Joseph Smith provided direct counsel. He said simply, "When I find out what God wants me to do, I do it!"

(Thomas S. Monson, *Be Your Best Self* [Salt Lake City: Deseret Book, 1979], 169.)

NOVEMBER 27
Learning to Love the Word of God

Therefore I love thy commandments above gold; yea, above fine gold.

Therefore I esteem all thy precepts concerning all things to be right; and I hate every false way.

Thy testimonies are wonderful: therefore doth my soul keep them.

The entrance of thy words giveth light; it giveth understanding unto the simple.

PSALM 119:127–30

See also 2 Ne. 4:15; Alma 17:2; JS—M 1:37.

I am grateful for emphasis on reading the scriptures. I hope that for you this will become something far more enjoyable than a duty; that, rather, it will become a love affair with the word of God. I promise you that as you read, your minds will be enlightened and your spirits will be lifted. At first it may seem tedious, but that will change into a wondrous experience with thoughts and words of things divine.

(Gordon B. Hinckley, *Teachings of Gordon B. Hinckley* [Salt Lake City: Deseret Book, 1997], 573–74.)

NOVEMBER 28
The Last Days

And I will shew wonders in the heavens and in the earth, blood, and fire, and pillars of smoke.

The sun shall be turned into darkness, and the moon into blood, before the great and the terrible day of the Lord come.

JOEL 2:30–31

See also Isa. 19:17; 24:20; Hag. 2:6; D&C 106:4; 110:16.

From these pleasant scenes our eyes are diverted to the world of wickedness of the last days. We are sickened at the sight of sin; we tremble as we see the plagues and pestilence and disasters and wars.

(Bruce R. McConkie, *The Millennial Messiah: The Second Coming of the Son of Man* [Salt Lake City: Deseret Book, 1982], 564.)

NOVEMBER 29
Prophecies Heralding the Second Coming

Behold, I will send my messenger, and he shall prepare the way before me: and the Lord, whom ye seek, shall suddenly come to his temple, even the messenger of the covenant, whom ye delight in: behold, he shall come, saith the Lord of hosts.

MALACHI 3:1

See also Job. 19:25; Ps. 102:16; D&C 86:4; 87:4; 133:37.

Just as all the prophecies heralding Christ's first advent were fulfilled, so will be all the prophecies heralding His second coming. Some of them may puzzle us, but increasingly it is possible to see through "glass, darkly" how such prophecies might come to pass.

(Neal A. Maxwell, *Wherefore, Ye Must Press Forward* [Salt Lake City: Deseret Book, 1977], 80.)

NOVEMBER 30
The Second Coming

Then shall the Lord go forth, and fight against those nations, as when he fought in the day of battle.

And his feet shall stand in that day upon the mount of Olives, which is before Jerusalem on the east, and the mount of Olives shall cleave in the midst thereof toward the east and toward the west, and there shall be a very great valley; and half of the mountain shall remove toward the north, and half of it toward the south.

ZECHARIAH 14:3–4

See also Dan.12:1; Micah 1:3; 1 Thes. 4:16; 2 Pet. 3:10.

I would venture a personal opinion that no event has occurred in all the history of the earth as dreadful as will be the day of the Second Coming—no event as fraught with the destructive forces of nature, as consequential for the nations of the earth, as terrible for the wicked, or as wonderful for the righteous.

(Gordon B. Hinckley, *Teachings of Gordon B. Hinckley* [Salt Lake City: Deseret Book, 1997], 575–76.)

DECEMBER

*If he call thee, . . . thou shalt say,
Speak, Lord; for thy servant heareath.*

—1 Samuel 3:9

DECEMBER 1
The Judgment Day

He shall call to the heavens from above, and to the earth, that he may judge his people.

PSALM 50:4

See also Eccl. 3:17; 11:9; 12:14; Amos 4:12; Mosiah 3:24.

Let us be sure we thoroughly understand the most important things we can do to prepare ourselves for our Lord's second coming to earth and, by our obedience and faithfulness, escape his punishment.

The following are important considerations. We must set our lives and homes in order. This means a searching of our souls, an admittance of wrongdoing, and repentance where needed. It means keeping all of God's commandments. It means loving our neighbor. It means living an exemplary life. It means being good husbands and wives. It means teaching and training our children in the ways of righteousness. It means being honest in all our doings, in business and at home. It means spreading the gospel of Jesus Christ to all the peoples of the world.

(Delbert L. Stapley, "To Make a People Prepared for the Lord," *Ensign*, Nov. 1975, 47.)

DECEMBER 2
Tithes and Offerings

Will a man rob God? Yet ye have robbed me. But ye say, Wherein have we robbed thee? In tithes and offerings.

Ye are cursed with a curse: for ye have robbed me, even this whole nation.

Bring ye all the tithes into the storehouse, that there may be meat in mine house, and prove me now herewith, saith the Lord of hosts, if I will not open you the windows of heaven, and pour you out a blessing, that there shall not be room enough to receive it.

MALACHI 3:8–10

See also Num. 18:26; Prov. 3:9; Luke 18:12; D&C 64:23.

They speak of robbing God and being cursed therefore, through failure to pay tithes and offerings, and of the temporal and spiritual blessings reserved for tithe payers. Those who walk mournfully before the Lord are promised great reward in due time . . . he will spare them in that day, and then shall all discern between the righteous and the wicked.

(Bruce R. McConkie, *The Mortal Messiah: From Bethlehem to Calvary* [Salt Lake City: Deseret Book, 1979–1981], 4:367.)

DECEMBER 3
Keys of the Sealing Power

Behold, I will send you Elijah the prophet before the coming of the great and dreadful day of the Lord:

And he shall turn the heart of the fathers to the children, and the heart of the children to their fathers, lest I come and smite the earth with a curse.

MALACHI 4:5–6

See also Isa. 22:22; Luke 1:17; 3 Ne. 25:5–6; D&C 2:1–3.

Many of you have already qualified for endowment in the temple, and others will have that great privilege yet in the future. In the temple, with the authority of the sealing power, blessings of the Abrahamic covenant will be conferred. There, we may truly become heirs to all the blessings of Abraham, Isaac, and Jacob.

(Russell M. Nelson, *Perfection Pending, and Other Favorite Discourses* [Salt Lake City: Deseret Book, 1998], 206.)

DECEMBER 4
Genealogy and Temple Work

And he shall sit as a refiner and purifier of silver: and he shall purify the sons of Levi, and purge them as gold and silver, that they may offer unto the Lord an offering in righteousness.

MALACHI 3:3

See also Isa. 56:5; Ezek. 43:11; Obad. 1:21; Moses 6:46.

We have asked the members of the Church to further the work of turning the hearts of the children to the fathers by getting their sacred family records in order. These records, including especially the "book containing the records of our dead," are a portion of the "offering in righteousness" referred to by Malachi, which we are to present in His holy temple, and without which we shall not abide the day of His coming.

(Spencer W. Kimball, *The Teachings of Spencer W. Kimball* [Salt Lake City: Bookcraft, 1982], 542–43.)

DECEMBER 5

Have Courage

Be strong and of a good courage, fear not, nor be afraid of them: for the Lord thy God, he it is that doth go with thee; he will not fail thee, nor forsake thee.

DEUTERONOMY 31:6

See also Josh. 23:6; 2 Sam 2:7; 1 Chr. 28:20; Ps. 27:14.

Without that personal witness they are ambivalent and unable to defend gospel truths or doctrines. It is people's incapacity to defend the faith, wrote George MacDonald, which can turn them into persecutors.

(Neal A. Maxwell, *That Ye May Believe* [Salt Lake City: Bookcraft, 1992], 102.)

DECEMBER 6
Our Redeemer

For thy Maker is thine husband; the Lord of hosts is his name; and thy Redeemer the Holy One of Israel; The God of the whole earth shall he be called.

ISAIAH 54:5

See also Isa. 43:3; D&C 76:1; Moses 1:6.

As Latter-day Saints, we know that whatsoever is truth is light. The source of this light is our Lord and Savior, Jesus Christ, who is "the light, and the life, and the truth of the world." In possessing this light, we can shine among our fellowmen through our lives and deeds, influencing them also to glorify our Father in Heaven.

(Joseph B. Wirthlin, *Finding Peace in Our Lives* [Salt Lake City: Deseret Book, 1995], 76.)

DECEMBER 7

Serve the Lord

Ye shall observe to do therefore as the Lord your God hath commanded you: ye shall not turn aside to the right hand or to the left.

Ye shall walk in all the ways which the Lord your God hath commanded you, that ye may live, and that it may be well with you, and that ye may prolong your days in the land which ye shall possess.

DEUTERONOMY 5:32–33

See also Deut. 10:12; 1 Sam. 15:22; 2 Chr. 8:14; Eccl. 12:13.

Now, you Latter-day Saints, what are you going to do now? As a result of this conference, we will be disappointed if we don't see an uplift among this people to serve the Lord better and to carry out more fully the Lord's mandate to us to love Him and serve Him by loving and serving our fellowmen.

(Harold B. Lee, *The Teachings of Harold B. Lee* [Salt Lake City: Bookcraft, 1996], 470.)

DECEMBER 8
Use Time Wisely

Whoso keepeth the commandment shall feel no evil thing: and a wise man's heart discerneth both time and judgment.

ECCLESIASTES 8:5

See also Ex. 21:19; Eccl. 3:1; Matt. 24:44; Hel. 13:38.

Jesus also taught us how important it is to use our time wisely. This does not mean there can never be any leisure, for there must be time for contemplation and for renewal, but there must be no waste of time. Wise time management is really the wise management of ourselves.

(Spencer W. Kimball, *The Teachings of Spencer W. Kimball* [Salt Lake City: Bookcraft, 1982], 482.)

DECEMBER 9
Teach and Share the Gospel

O Zion, that bringest good tidings, get thee up into the high mountain; O Jerusalem, that bringest good tidings, lift up thy voice with strength; lift it up, be not afraid; say unto the cities of Judah, Behold your God!

Isaiah 40:9

See also Isa. 52:7; 61:1; D&C 19:29; 38:41.

We continually strive to share the gospel with others, but we cannot dilute it to suit their taste. We did not set the standards; the Lord did. It is His church. . . .

Therefore, missionary work is not casual; it is very determined.

(Boyd K. Packer, *Let Not Your Heart Be Troubled* [Salt Lake City: Bookcraft, 1991], 176.)

DECEMBER 10
Seek to Serve

And the people served the Lord all the days of Joshua, and all the days of the elders that outlived Joshua, who had seen all the great works of the Lord, that he did for Israel.

JUDGES 2:7

See also Deut. 11:13–15; Josh. 24:15; Matt. 20:27; Mosiah 8:18.

We must not let our lives fall below Church standards so that we get "past feeling" so far as the Spirit of the Lord is concerned or so far as our awareness of the feelings of those we seek to lead and to serve. We need not be intimidated or deterred from pursuing the right course by the feelings of followers when they err, but we can help them more if we are sensitive to their needs, and the Spirit can help us so to be.

(Harold B. Lee, *The Teachings of Harold B. Lee* [Salt Lake City: Bookcraft, 1996], 509.)

DECEMBER 11
Follow Our Savior

The Lord is my light and my salvation; whom shall I fear? the Lord is the strength of my life; of whom shall I be afraid?

PSALM 27:1

See also Isa. 2:5; 9:2; 60:19; Luke 18:22; 3 Ne. 27:27.

Those whose goal it is to follow the Savior straightway not only look for answers to their own problems but also help others find solutions to life's difficulties. They open their hearts and minds to those who are troubled, ignored, or weary.

(Marvin J. Ashton, *Be of Good Cheer* [Salt Lake City: Deseret Book, 1987], 59.)

DECEMBER 12
Gratitude to the Lord

It is a good thing to give thanks unto the Lord, and to sing praises unto thy name, O most High:

To shew forth thy lovingkindness in the morning, and thy faithfulness every night,

PSALM 92:1–2

See also 1 Chr. 23:30; Pss. 50:14; 136:1; 1 Cor. 15:57.

I don't believe it's possible to overdo gratitude with the Lord. He gives us so many blessings (most of which we're not even aware of) that I don't think we can ever thank him enough.

(Gene R. Cook, *Receiving Answers to Our Prayers* [Salt Lake City: Deseret Book, 1996], 65.)

DECEMBER 13
Christ the Vicarious Redeemer

For their redeemer is mighty; he shall plead their cause with thee.

PROVERBS 23:11

See also Job 19:25; Isa. 41:14; 1 Pet. 1:18–20; Ether 3:14.

Vicarious work, when authorized of God, is acceptable to him. This should not startle the Christian mind, when it is remembered that the whole fabric of Christianity rests upon the vicarious work done by Jesus Christ for the redemption and salvation of those who were powerless to redeem and save themselves. Men cannot answer by proxy for the deeds done in the body, but there have always been ceremonies in the Church of Christ that one person might perform for another. The priest who ministers in behalf of the people is a type of the Great Mediator, "our only access unto God."

(Orson F. Whitney, *Gospel Themes* [Salt Lake City, 1914], 52.)

DECEMBER 14
Testimony of the Savior

❦

For I know that my redeemer liveth, and that he shall stand at the latter day upon the earth:

And though after my skin worms destroy this body, yet in my flesh shall I see God.

JOB 19:25–26

See also John 17:3; 1 Cor. 12:3; Moro. 10:4; D&C 46:13.

Our testimony meetings need to be more centered on the Savior, the doctrines of the gospel, the blessings of the Restoration, and the teachings of the scriptures. We need to replace stories, travelogues, and lectures with pure testimonies. Those who are entrusted to speak and teach in our meetings need to do so with doctrinal power that will be both heard and felt, lifting the spirits and edifying our people. You will remember at the heart of King Benjamin's powerful sermon to his people was his personal witness of the Savior, who at that time had yet to be born into mortality.

(M. Russell Ballard, "Pure Testimony," *Ensign,* Nov. 2004, 41.)

DECEMBER 15
Come to the Tree of Life

But because the Lord loved you, and because he would keep the oath which he had sworn unto your fathers, hath the Lord brought you out with a mighty hand, and redeemed you out of the house of bondmen, from the hand of Pharaoh king of Egypt.

DEUTERONOMY 7:8

See also Deut. 7:13; 10:15, 18; 23:5; Mal. 1:2.

In Lehi's vision of the tree of life, he saw a man dressed in a white robe who beckoned him to follow him through the dark and dreary waste, which represented the temptations of the world. With the help of prayer, Lehi was led to partake of the fruit of that tree, which provided him "with exceeding great joy." We would hope that you teachers would be as men in white robes, leading our youth safely through the temptations of the world so that they too may partake of the tree of life and have exceeding great joy.

(Ezra Taft Benson, *The Teachings of Ezra Taft Benson* [Salt Lake City: Bookcraft, 1988], 312.)

DECEMBER 16

Remember, Oh Remember

Remember his marvellous works that he hath done, his wonders, and the judgments of his mouth.

1 CHRONICLES 16:12

See also Neh. 1:8; Ps. 63:6; Mosiah 4:11; Hel. 5:5–9, 12.

How can you and I remember, always, the goodness of God, that we can retain a remission of our sins? The Apostle John recorded what the Savior taught us of a gift of remembrance which comes through the gift of the Holy Ghost: "But the Comforter, which is the Holy Ghost, whom the Father will send in my name, he shall teach you all things, and bring all things to your remembrance, whatsoever I have said unto you."

(Henry B. Eyring, *To Draw Closer to God: A Collection of Discourses* [Salt Lake City: Deseret Book, 1997], 77–78.)

DECEMBER 17
Become Like Our Savior Jesus Christ

Thou shalt be perfect with the Lord thy God.

DEUTERONOMY 18:13

See also Gen. 17:1; Job 1:1; Pss. 37:37; 101:6; 3 Ne. 12:48.

The grand object of our coming to this earth is that we may become like Christ, for if we are not like him, we cannot become the sons of God, and be joint heirs with Christ.

(Joseph F. Smith, *Gospel Doctrine: Selections from the Sermons and Writings of Joseph F. Smith* [Salt Lake City: Deseret Book, 1939], 18.)

DECEMBER 18
Clean Hands and a Pure Heart

He that hath clean hands, and a pure heart; who hath not lifted up his soul unto vanity, nor sworn deceitfully.

He shall receive the blessing from the Lord, and righteousness from the God of his salvation.

PSALM 24:4–5

See also Ps. 73:1; Isa.1:16; 52:11; Jer. 4:14; 1 Pet. 1:22.

We must strive to be pure in thought and action.

It is impressive to me that the primary requirement of the Lord for the work of his ministry is personal purity. To the first elders of the Church, the Lord said:

"Sanctify yourselves; yea, purify your hearts, and cleanse your hands and your feet before me, that I may make you clean."

(Howard W. Hunter, *The Teachings of Howard W. Hunter* [Salt Lake City: Bookcraft, 1997], 75.)

DECEMBER 19
Reverence the Lord

And the Lord commanded us to do all these statutes, to fear the Lord our God, for our good always,
that he might preserve us alive, as it is at this day.

DEUTERONOMY 6:24

See also Gen. 42:18; Lev. 26:2; Job 28:28; Heb. 12:28.

There are wide areas of our society from which
the spirit of prayer and reverence and worship has
vanished. . . . Unfortunately we sometimes find
this lack of reverence even within the Church.
Occasionally we visit too loudly, enter and leave
meetings too disrespectfully in what should be an
hour of prayer and purifying worship. Reverence is
the atmosphere of heaven.

(Howard W. Hunter, *The Teachings of Howard W. Hunter*
[Salt Lake City: Bookcraft, 1997], 103.)

DECEMBER 20
Self-Mastery

He that hath no rule over his own spirit is like a city that is broken down, and without walls.

PROVERBS 25:28

See also Pss. 37:8; 119:101; Prov. 14:29; Alma 38:12.

A purpose of this probationary state is that man learns to control all of his bodily appetites, desires, and passions. . . . Our aim should be to become fully masters of our bodies.

(Ezra Taft Benson, *The Teachings of Ezra Taft Benson* [Salt Lake City: Bookcraft, 1988], 445.)

DECEMBER 21
Increase Your Faith in Jesus Christ

Then was the king exceeding glad for him, and commanded that they should take Daniel up out of the den. So Daniel was taken up out of the den, and no manner of hurt was found upon him, because he believed in his God.

DANIEL 6:23

See also 2 Chr. 20:20; Nahum 1:7; Hab. 2:4; Hel. 3:35.

The seed is the word of God. It must be planted in the heart of the person you serve and whose faith you want to see increase. [Alma] described what must happen this way: "Now, we will compare the word unto a seed. Now, if ye give place, that a seed may be planted in your heart, behold, if it be a true seed, or a good seed, if ye do not cast it out by your unbelief, that ye will resist the Spirit of the Lord, behold, it will begin to swell within your breasts; and when you feel these swelling motions, ye will begin to say within yourselves—It must needs be that this is a good seed, or that the word is good, for it beginneth to enlarge my soul."

(Henry B. Eyring, *To Draw Closer to God: A Collection of Discourses* [Salt Lake City: Deseret Book, 1997], 185.)

DECEMBER 22
The Pure in Heart

Depart ye, depart ye, go ye out from thence, touch no unclean thing; go ye out of the midst of her; be ye clean, that bear the vessels of the Lord.

ISAIAH 52:11

See also Pss. 24:4; 73:1; Acts 15:9; James 4:8; D&C 88:74.

The pure in heart have a distinctive way of looking at life. Their attitudes and desires cause them to view their experiences in terms of eternity. This eternal perspective affects their choices and priorities. As they draw farther from worldliness they feel closer to our Father in Heaven and more able to be guided by his Spirit. We call this state of mind, this quality of life, spirituality.

Spirituality is a lens through which we view life and a gauge by which we evaluate it.

(Dallin H. Oaks, *Pure in Heart* [Salt Lake City: Bookcraft, 1988], 111.)

DECEMBER 23
The Prophet Joseph Smith

And the book is delivered to him that is not learned, saying, Read this, I pray thee: and he saith, I am not learned.

ISAIAH 29:12

See also 2 Ne. 3:7, 15; D&C 21:4–6.

Joseph Smith, the Prophet and Seer of the Lord, has done more, save Jesus only, for the salvation of men in this world, than any other man that ever lived in it. In the short space of twenty years, he has brought forth the Book of Mormon . . . has sent the fulness of the everlasting gospel, which it contained, to the four quarters of the earth; . . . and like most of the Lord's anointed in ancient times, has sealed his mission and his works with his own blood; and so has his brother Hyrum. In life they were not divided, and in death they were not separated!

(John Taylor, in Doctrine & Covenants 135:3.)

DECEMBER 24
The Purest Motive

Commit thy works unto the Lord, and thy thoughts shall be established.

See also Prov. 23:7; Rom. 13:10; 2 Ne. 26:24; Moro. 7:5–11.

We can work to reform our motives if we are continually asking ourselves: Why am I taking this action? That question is especially important for actions that we suppose to be good. It reminds us that it is not enough to act in ways that seem to be good. We must act for the right reasons. If we truly desire to please God and serve him, continual self-examination of our reasons for actions cannot fail to expose our selfish and sordid motives and challenge us to reform them.

The ultimate good motive for any act is charity—the pure love of Christ. We acquire that motive in two ways: (1) by praying for love, and (2) by practicing service.

(Dallin H. Oaks, *Pure in Heart* [Salt Lake City: Bookcraft, 1988], 148.)

DECEMBER 25
Prophecies of Jesus Christ

But thou, Beth-lehem Ephratah, though thou be little among the thousands of Judah, yet out of thee shall he come forth unto me that is to be ruler in Israel; whose goings forth have been from of old, from everlasting.

MICAH 5:2

See also Isa. 7:14; Jer. 23:5; Zech. 9:9.

One has but to read again the prophetic words of the Lord to Adam, Jacob, Abraham, and Moses, and to many others, to know that the Lord has sent into the world in every dispensation and in preparation for His advent the sure knowledge of who He was and of His mission for the redemption of mankind through the plan of salvation, by which all may be saved by obedience to the laws and ordinances of the gospel.

(Harold B. Lee, *The Teachings of Harold B. Lee* [Salt Lake City: Bookcraft, 1996], 12.)

DECEMBER 26
Suffering of the Lord

Surely he hath borne our griefs, and carried our sorrows: yet we did esteem him stricken, smitten of God, and afflicted.

But he was wounded for our transgressions, he was bruised for our iniquities: the chastisement of our peace was upon him; and with his stripes we are healed.

All we like sheep have gone astray; we have turned every one to his own way; and the Lord hath laid on him the iniquity of us all.

ISAIAH 53:4–6

See also Lev. 17:11; Isa. 63:9; Alma 7:11; 11:40; Hel.5:9.

It was in Gethsemane that Jesus took on Himself the sins of the world, in Gethsemane that His pain was equivalent to the cumulative burden of all men, in Gethsemane that He descended below all things so that all could repent and come to Him. The mortal mind fails to fathom, the tongue cannot express, the pen of man cannot describe the breadth, the depth, the height of the suffering of our Lord—nor His infinite love for us.

(Ezra Taft Benson, *The Teachings of Ezra Taft Benson* [Salt Lake City: Bookcraft, 1988], 14.)

DECEMBER 27
Seek After the Lost Souls

I looked on my right hand, and beheld, but there was no man that would know me. refuge failed me; no man cared for my soul.

PSALM 142:4

See also Isa. 1:18; Ezek 18:22; Mosiah 28:3.

The Lost Sheep, The Lost Coin, The Prodigal Son. The first was lost in his eagerness to seek daily sustenance and wandered too far from the flock. The coin was lost through carelessness of the housewife. The prodigal son became lost because he desired his portion and spent it in profligacy. He did not get it back until he came to himself and said, "I will rise and go to my father." Through study and prayer to the best of your ability counter-act those three enticing elements as you seek to bring back the lost ones.

(David O. McKay, *Gospel Ideals: Selections from the Discourses of David O. McKay* [Salt Lake City: Improvement Era, 1953], 220–21.)

DECEMBER 28
The Golden Rule

But the stranger that dwelleth with you shall be unto you as one born among you, and thou shalt love him as thyself; for ye were strangers in the land of Egypt: I am the Lord your God.

LEVITICUS 19:34

See also Luke 6:31; 1 Cor. 16:14; D&C 112:11.

"Remember the worth of souls is great." A proper conception of this divine principle would change the attitude of the world to the benefit and happiness of all human beings. It would bring into active operation the Golden Rule: Do unto others as you would have others do unto you.

(David O. McKay, *Gospel Ideals: Selections from the Discourses of David O. McKay* [Salt Lake City: Improvement Era, 1953], 347.)

DECEMBER 29
Punished for Our Own Sins

According to their deeds, accordingly he will repay, fury to his adversaries, recompence to his enemies; to the islands he will repay recompence.

ISAIAH 59:18

See also Gen. 9:6; Deut. 24:16; 2 Kgs. 14:6; Mosiah 2:33.

We may sin or live righteously, but we cannot escape responsibility. To blame our sins upon the Lord, saying they are inherent and cannot be controlled, is cheap and cowardly. To blame our sins upon our parents and our upbringing is the way of the escapist. One's parents may have failed; our own backgrounds may have been frustrating, but as sons and daughters of a living God we have within ourselves the power to rise above our circumstances, to change our lives. Man can change human nature. Man must transform his life. We will be punished for our sins. We must accept responsibility for our sins. We can overcome. We must control and master ourselves.

(Spencer W. Kimball, *Faith Precedes the Miracle* [Salt Lake City: Deseret Book, 1972], 175–76.)

DECEMBER 30
Overcoming Weaknesses through the Lord

God is my strength and power: and he maketh my way perfect.

2 Samuel 22:33

See also Pss. 71:16; 118:14; 2 Ne. 22:2; Alma 26:11–12.

Coming to earth was part of God's plan for eternal progress. Mortality was intended by God to be a short duration in which men could prove themselves to see if they would do all that the Lord commanded. While here, we receive a body, experience trial, and learn to overcome weaknesses associated with our physical bodies. We are here to learn self-mastery. By learning to govern our natures, our appetites and passions, we draw closer to the divine nature of God, thereby fulfilling the mandate of the Master to "be . . . perfect, even as [our] Father which is in heaven is perfect."

(Ezra Taft Benson, *Come unto Christ* [Salt Lake City: Deseret Book, 1983], 74–75.)

DECEMBER 31
Organize Every Needful Thing

And there is nothing that the Lord thy God shall take in his heart to do but what he will do it.

ABRAHAM 3:17

See also Prov. 1:8; 4:13; Dan. 1:17; Mosiah 4:27.

A prerequisite for "doing" is goal setting. Actions are preceded by thoughts and planning. All of us must take charge of our own lives. We must evaluate the choices that are open to us, and then we must act positively on our own decision. An old proverb states, "A journey of one thousand miles begins with the first step." The word *straightway* suggests the urgency to take that first step toward any worthy goal.

(Marvin J. Ashton, *Be of Good Cheer* [Salt Lake City: Deseret Book, 1987], 56–57.)

Thematic Index

THEME   DAYS

Adversity 8.8

Affliction 3.26

Appetite, Overcome A. or Worldly Pleasures . 4.10

Armour of God, Put on the 6.14

Atonement 3.28, 3.29

Attitude 8.5

Becoming Like the Lord 10.13

Blessings 1.29, 2.1, 3.3, 4.2, 4.9, 8.12,
    10.5, 11.4, 11.11

Book of Mormon 1.6, 2.6

Build Up the Kingdom of God 10.2

Build upon the Rock 4.29

Callings 9.8, 10.23

Care for Others 6.25

Charity. 2.19

Chastening. 4.20

Chastity 6.15

Children. 1.30, 8.1

Choose to Serve the Lord. 5.7

Christ. 3.30, 4.15, 3.28, 9.11, 9.30, 10.26,
   10.29, 11.23 12.6, 12.13, 12.17

Church in the Latter Days 11.18

Cleave to the Lord 5.5

Come unto Christ 4.15

Commandments 2.10, 4.24, 8.25, 8.26, 10.3, 11.9

Communication with God. 5.26

Contention. 2.19

Contrite Spirit, Broken Heart and 12.26

Courage 5.2, 11.12, 12.5

Covenant, Abrahamic 2.14, 2.23

Covenant, New and Everlasting. 3.10

Covenants 2.15, 2.16, 2.17, 2.18, 3.5, 3.6,
3.31, 4.1, 4.2, 4.30, 7.28, 8.23, 10.19

Creation. 1.3, 1.5, 1.15, 1.17, 1.20, 6.19

Defend the Faith 12.5

Destroy the Wicked, the L. will 2.9, 2.24

Devil 1.22, 1.23, 1.27

Diligence 5.17

Endure to the End 8.11, 10.11

Enmity Between Mankind and Satan 1.23

Envy 3.13, 3.16

Eternal Marriage 3.9, 3.10

Evil 9.9

Example 4.22, 5.22, 7.3

Faith 2.4, 11.5, 12.21

Fall 1.26

Family 1.18

Fast 10.4, 10.5

Fear 4.13, 7.23, 8.16

Feast Upon the Word 4.15, 11.25

Follow 5.6, 5.29, 7.16, 12.11

Foreordination 1.8, 10.9

Forgiveness 3.23, 6.3, 8.27

Freedom 7.4

Friendship 5.10, 6.5, 8.4

Gathering of Israel 10.16

Genealogy 12.4

Gifts of the Spirit. 6.29

Glory of God. 1.4

Glory of the Lord in the Temple 10.31

God 1.1,1.4,1.8, 1.9, 1.10, 1.13, 1.17,
    1.21, 2.11, 2.20, 2.22, 3.1, 4.16, 5.11, 5.21,
    5.23, 5.26, 6.4, 6.14, 6.20, 6.22, 6.27, 7.10,
    7.17, 7.29, 8.18, 9.11, 9.19,10.2, 10.7, 10.12,
    10.21, 11.8, 11.17, 11.27

Good Works 3.20, 9.5

Gospel 1.29, 2.2, 2.7, 8.14, 12.9

Gossip 11.15

Gratitude 7.24, 9.29, 12.12

Hearkening 2.11, 7.29, 8.30, 10.21

Heart, Beware of Hard H. 11.14

Help, Pray for H. in all Things 4.3, 7.30

Heritage. 3.7

Holy Ghost 2.1

Honesty 5.19

Honor 2.17, 4.23, 5.23, 9.8

Hope 9.1, 9.27

House of the Lord 6.24, 10.30

Humility 5.30

Immorality, Consequences of. 3.17

Influences of the World, Resisting the 11.7

Israel, Shepherd of 10.17

Jealousy 6.8

Jesus Christ 1.3, 1.15, 2.17, 4.28, 9.29,
    10.17, 12.17, 12.21, 12.25

Joseph Smith 12.23

Joy 1.18, 3.11, 10.8

Judgment. 12.1

Justification 1.31

Kindness 5.18

Kingdom of God 10.2, 11.17, 11.19

Know God. 1.1

Knowledge and Wisdom 8.6

Last Days. 9.4, 11.28

Last Pruning of the Vineyard. 8.20

Latter Days 2.6, 10.18, 10.20, 11.18, 11.19

Laws of the Lord 10.4, 11.2

Leadership 4.8, 7.6, 7.7, 7.8, 7.9, 10.25, 11.2

Life 1.11, 3.26, 3.30, 8.7, 12.15

Light 8.19, 12.18

Listen while You Pray 5.27

Look to God and Live 4.16

Lord 2.11, 2.22, 2.24, 2.27, 2.28, 3.8, 3.14,
    3.25, 3.27 3.28, 3.30, 4.3, 4.4, 4.5, 4.6, 4.7,
    4.18, 4.19, 4.20 4.23, 4.25, 4.26, 5.1, 5.3,
    5.4, 5.5, 5.6, 5.7., 5.8, 5.9, 5.12, 5.20, 5.24,
    5.31, 6.1, 6.21, 6.23, 6.24, 7.2, 7.12, 7.14,
    7.18, 7.28, 8.9, 8.13, 8.21, 8.22, 8.29, 8.31, 9.1,
    9.10, 9.18, 9.20, 9.21, 9.22, 9.23, 9.24, 10.3,
    10.6, 10.7, 10.10, 10.13, 10.17, 10.22, 10.30,
    10.31, 11.2, 11.11, 12.6, 12.7, 12.12

Lost 9.22, 12.27

Love 3.24, 4.20, 5.15, 6.11, 7.9, 8.22, 11.27, 12.24

Loyalty 5.10

Mankind 1.23, 2.25

Marriage 1.21, 3.5, 3.9, 3.10

Meekness 4.14

Mercy. 6.22, 8.21

Millennium—A Time of Peace and Joy. 10.8

Miracles 5.11, 7.21

Missionary Work 8.16, 8.19, 10.18

Mothers 5.14

Mount Zion, Saviors on. 10.1

Murmur Not 4.11

Neighbor, Be a Good N. 7.25

New Jerusalem 2.6

Obedience 1.25, 2.10, 3.2, 3.3, 4.9, 4.17, 4.18, 5.9, 6.2, 6.18, 11.11

Offerings 2.21, 2.28, 12.2

Old Testament. 9.19

Opposition 10.11

Organize Every Needful Thing 12.31

Overcoming. 3.15, 4.13, 6.8, 7.23, 7.31

Parent, Love of a 3.24

Paths 9.17

Peace 7.15

Penitent, The Lord Forgives the Sins of the P.9.23

Personal Revelation 11.14

Plan of Salvation 1.30, 9.25

Positive Attitude. 8.5

Power . 2.4, 4.22, 5.22, 7.17, 7.20, 7.22, 8.10, 12.3

Prayer. . . 1.2, 1.7, 1.9, 2.13, 5.27, 7.22, 7.30, 11.10

Preach 2.2, 8.16, 8.18, 10.14

Preparing 10.7, 12.1

Pride 7.31

Priesthood 3.4, 7.20

Proclaim the Gospel. 8.14, 8.16

Prophecy 3.21, 11.29

Prophets 5.29, 7.16, 7.18, 7.19, 8.29, 8.30, 10.14

Provide, the Lord Will P. 3.1, 4.4

Pruning the Vineyard. 8.20

Record Keeping 2.3

Redeemer. 12.6, 12.13

Remember 2.16, 4.5, 4.24, 4.30, 6.4, 12.16

Renewing Our Covenants 4.1

Repentance 1.28, 2.8, 8.15, 10.14, 10.27

Resurrection. 9.14

Revelation 3.19, 11.13

Righteousness. . . 2.12, 3.18, 5.16, 8.10, 11.4, 11.6

Rock of Our Salvation 4.28, 4.29

Sabbath 1.19, 7.13

Sacrament 3.31

Sacrifice 5.16, 6.2

Saints of the Latter Days 10.20

Sanctification 1.31, 5.4

Satan 1.14, 1.22, 1.23, 1.27

Saved, Repent and Be S. 1.28

Savior 9.11, 9.12, 9.13, 9.14, 9.15, 9.17,
    9.18, 9.29 9.30, 10.17, 12.6,12.11,12.14, 12.17

Saviors on Mount Zion 10.1

Scriptures. 8.28, 11.26

Sealing Power, Keys of the 12.3

Second Coming 10.6, 11.29, 11.30

Second Estate. 1.12

Serve 5.7, 7.14, 7.28, 10.9, 10.10, 10.24, 12.7,12.10

Service, Temple 7.27, 11.5

Share the Gospel 12.9

Shepherd of Israel 10.17, 10.26

Sin 4.21, 6.16, 9.5, 9.23, 10.28

Smith, Joseph. 12.23

Spirit 3.19, 6.29, 9.2

Spirit Prison. 9.12

Spiritual Wealth. 7.1

Strength1.7, 5.12, 5.31, 6.6, 8.9, 9.20, 10.10, 10.12

Submit Your Will to the Lord 4.19

Teach 1.30, 5.24, 7.3, 7.6, 8.1, 8.18, 11.23

Temple. 5.20, 5.21, 6.24, 7.26, 7.27, 10.30,
    10.31, 11.1, 11.3, 12.4

Temple Marriage 3.5, 3.9, 3.10

Temptation 3.15, 4.21, 4.27, 6.13

Testify 11.23

Testimony 6.13, 8.17, 12.14

Thanksgiving. 11.24

Time 8.2, 12.8

Tithes and Offerings 2.21, 12.2

Tribulation. 3.14

Trust in the Lord 3.27, 6.1, 6.23, 10.22

Truth 11.6

Values 5.28

Weaknesses 12.30

Wicked 2.9, 2.24

Will of God 1.10, 1.13, 4.19

Wisdom 6.10, 6.27, 6.30, 7.8, 8.6, 12.8

Word of God 1.6, 1.24, 4.15, 4.17, 6.20, 7.29,
    8.18, 10.12, 10.21, 11.25, 11.27

Work and Glory of God 1.4

World 2.25, 5.13, 11.7

Worldliness 2.20, 4.10, 10.15

Worship 2.26, 11.8

Youth. 5.24

Zion. 2.5, 10.1, 11.20, 11.21, 12.22

About the Authors

Ed J. Pinegar

Ed Pinegar is a retired dentist and long-time teacher of early-morning seminary and religion classes at Brigham Young University. He teaches at the Joseph Smith Academy and has served as a mission president in England and at the Missionary Training Center in Provo, Utah. He has been a bishop twice and a stake president and is a temple sealer. Ed and his wife, Patricia, are the parents of eight children and reside in Orem, Utah.

Richard J. Allen

Richard Allen is a husband, father, teacher, and writer. He has served on several high councils, in several stake presidencies, and as a bishop. Richard's teaching assignments in the Church have included service as a full-time missionary, instructor in various priesthood quorums, gospel doctrine teacher, and stake institute director. He has served as a faculty member at both Brigham Young University and Johns Hopkins University. Richard has coauthored many articles, manuals, and books and has served on a number of national educational boards. He and his wife, Carol Lynn Hansen Allen, have four children and five grandchildren.